JEREMIAH
BIBLE STUDY SERIES

MATTHEW

THE ARRIVAL OF THE KING

DR. DAVID JEREMIAH

Prepared by Hudson Bible

THOMAS NELSON
Since 1798

MATTHEW
JEREMIAH BIBLE STUDY SERIES

© 2019 by Dr. David Jeremiah

Published in Nashville, Tennessee, by Thomas Nelson. Thomas Nelson is a registered trademark of HarperCollins Christian Publishing, Inc.

Produced with the assistance of Hudson Bible (www.HudsonBible.com). Project staff include Christopher D. Hudson and Randy Southern.

The quote by Papias in the Introduction is from Eusebius, *History of the Church*, 3:39. The quote by Irenaeus is from *Against Heresies*, 3:1. The quote by Origen is from Eusebius, *History of the Church*, 6:25.

Thomas Nelson titles may be purchased in bulk for educational, business, fundraising, or sales promotional use. For information, please e-mail SpecialMarkets@ThomasNelson.com.

ISBN 978-0-310-09149-3

SECOND Printing JULY 2020 / Printed in the United States of America

CONTENTS

INTRODUCTION TO
The Gospel of Matthew

"As Jesus passed on from there, He saw a man named Matthew sitting at the tax office. And He said to him, 'Follow Me.' So he arose and followed Him" (Matthew 9:9). At first glance, it seems surprising that Jesus would call a man like Matthew (also known as Levi) to become one of His disciples. As a small-time tax collector, Matthew would have been despised by the Jewish people, who viewed those in the profession as traitors to Rome. But the fact that Matthew was educated, literate, and also familiar with Jewish law and customs made him the ideal candidate to not only accompany Jesus during His earthly ministry but also record all that he witnessed. The result is the Gospel we have today—a document that since its creation has been read, studied, memorized, and treasured throughout church history in every part of the world.

AUTHOR AND DATE

The Gospel of Matthew, as with the other three Gospels, does not list the name of its author. However, the earliest church fathers to mention the Gospel all concurred it was written by the disciple named Matthew. Papias, who lived c. AD 60–163, wrote, "Matthew composed the *Logia* [Gospel] in the Hebrew dialect, and everyone interpreted them as he was able." Irenaeus (c. AD 130–202) wrote, "Matthew also issued a written Gospel among the Hebrews in their own dialect." Origen (c. AD 185–254) agreed, stating, "Among the four Gospels . . . I have learned by tradition that the first was written by Matthew, who was once a publican, but afterwards an apostle of Jesus Christ." Internal evidence indicates the Gospel was likely written sometime between AD 50 to 60, possibly from Antioch.

BACKGROUND AND SETTING

While Matthew does not overtly state his purpose in writing his Gospel, it is clear his intended audience was predominantly Jewish and that his overriding goal was to demonstrate that Jesus—the carpenter from Nazareth—was their long-awaited Messiah. This is seen in the fact that Matthew references Jewish customs without explaining them, frequently cites prophecies from the Old Testament to show how Jesus fulfilled them, refers to Jesus as "the Son of David," and uses the phrase "kingdom of heaven" rather than "kingdom of God" so as not to offend those Jews who believed it was sacrilegious to speak or write God's name. Matthew's genealogy goes back only as far as Abraham, the father of the Jewish race, and his account of Jesus' ministry focuses more on Christ's work within Galilee than among the Gentiles.

KEY THEMES

Several key themes are prominent in Matthew's Gospel. The first, as previously noted, is that Jesus was *the promised Messiah* whose birth, ministry, death, and resurrection were prophesied in the Old Testament. Matthew makes his case by quoting more than sixty prophecies from the Old Testament, revealing how Jesus fulfilled each one. Matthew's use of the "Son of David" for Jesus, in addition to his narrative on the Magi who presented gifts to him, reveal that he intended to present Jesus as the true King of the Jewish people.

A second theme is that *Jesus ushered in a new kingdom.* Jesus provided the first glimpse of this new kingdom in His Sermon on the Mount (see Matthew 5–7) . . . and it was not at all what the Jewish people were expecting. This "kingdom of heaven" that Jesus proclaimed was both a present reality (as Jesus revealed through the healings He performed) and a future hope (which He depicted in many of His teachings and parables). Throughout Matthew's Gospel, we find Jesus instructing His followers on what living in this type of kingdom required from them.

A third theme is that *Jesus was a teacher and worker of miracles.* Matthew records five major discourses from Jesus (5–7; 10; 13; 18–20; 24; 25), each followed by narratives of Jesus' works. These works often took the form of miracles that Jesus performed—signs that revealed how Jesus was the promised Messiah and was ushering in the arrival of God's kingdom on earth. Jesus' acts over nature (such as the calming of the sea and the multiplication of loaves and fish to feed crowds of people) in particular point to His authority as the Messiah.

A fourth theme is that *Jesus warned about the danger of unbelief.* Matthew often shows Jesus engaging with the Pharisees and Sadducees—the Jewish religious leaders of the day—to show how their use of rituals and traditions were keeping the people from finding God. This culminates with Jesus issuing seven "woes" against such teachers (see Matthew 23:13–30). Many of Jesus' parables also illustrate how the Jewish people were closed to receiving His words. Jesus repeatedly warned of the failure to act on the message He was proclaiming.

KEY APPLICATIONS

Matthew shows how Jesus, as the promised Messiah, is worthy of our *hope.* He shows how Jesus, as the Messiah, is worthy of our *trust.* And he explains how Jesus, as the eternal King, is worthy of our complete *devotion* . . . and our complete *submission* to Him.

THE MAKING OF A MESSIAH

Matthew 1:1–2:23

GETTING STARTED

What is your favorite part of the Christmas story? Why do you like that part?

_____

_____

_____

_____

_____

_____

_____

_____

_____

_____

_____

_____

_____

_____

_____

_____

_____

_____

_____

_____

SETTING THE STAGE

For 400 years God had been silent. The books of what we know as the Old Testament were completed, and nothing new had been added to their ranks. The silence was ultimately broken by a tax collector, of all people. Guided by the Holy Spirit, a man named Matthew began his account of Jesus' life with a genealogy.

The disciple of Christ had a specific intent in writing his Gospel: he wanted to prove to his Jewish readers that Jesus was *their* Messiah. The first step in that process was to trace Jesus' earthly lineage and demonstrate His claim to the throne of Israel. So Matthew begins his genealogy with Abraham, the father of the Jewish people. He follows Jesus' ancestry through King David. To emphasize the connection with the beloved monarch, Matthew refers to Jesus as the "Son of David" several times in his Gospel. From David, Matthew traces Jesus' royal ancestry through Zedekiah, the last king of Judah, all the way to Jesus' earthly father, Joseph.

The narrative that follows begins with a young couple in crisis. Joseph and Mary were pledged to be married, but the most extraordinary event in human history interrupted their plans. Mary learned that she had been chosen to give birth to the Messiah. Although she was still a virgin, the Holy Spirit had planted a seed within her. She was pregnant.

Joseph knew that Mary's child was not his, so he was faced with a dilemma. His first instinct was to resolve the matter quietly by giving Mary a divorce. But a visit from an angel convinced him to change his mind and embrace his role as Jesus' earthly father.

EXPLORING THE TEXT

The Genealogy of Jesus the Messiah (Matthew 1:1–17)

¹ The book of the genealogy of Jesus Christ, the Son of David, the Son of Abraham:

[2] Abraham begot Isaac, Isaac begot Jacob, and Jacob begot Judah and his brothers. [3] Judah begot Perez and Zerah by Tamar, Perez begot Hezron, and Hezron begot Ram. [4] Ram begot Amminadab, Amminadab begot Nahshon, and Nahshon begot Salmon. [5] Salmon begot Boaz by Rahab, Boaz begot Obed by Ruth, Obed begot Jesse, [6] and Jesse begot David the king.

David the king begot Solomon by her who had been the wife of Uriah. [7] Solomon begot Rehoboam, Rehoboam begot Abijah, and Abijah begot Asa. [8] Asa begot Jehoshaphat, Jehoshaphat begot Joram, and Joram begot Uzziah. [9] Uzziah begot Jotham, Jotham begot Ahaz, and Ahaz begot Hezekiah. [10] Hezekiah begot Manasseh, Manasseh begot Amon, and Amon begot Josiah. [11] Josiah begot Jeconiah and his brothers about the time they were carried away to Babylon.

[12] And after they were brought to Babylon, Jeconiah begot Shealtiel, and Shealtiel begot Zerubbabel. [13] Zerubbabel begot Abiud, Abiud begot Eliakim, and Eliakim begot Azor. [14] Azor begot Zadok, Zadok begot Achim, and Achim begot Eliud. [15] Eliud begot Eleazar, Eleazar begot Matthan, and Matthan begot Jacob. [16] And Jacob begot Joseph the husband of Mary, of whom was born Jesus who is called Christ.

[17] So all the generations from Abraham to David are fourteen generations, from David until the captivity in Babylon are fourteen generations, and from the captivity in Babylon until the Christ are fourteen generations.

---

1. Matthew lists five women in Jesus' ancestry, which was unusual for genealogies of the time. Why do you think Matthew included Tamar, Rahab, Ruth, Bathsheba, and Mary in his list of Jesus' ancestors (see verses 3, 5–6, 16)?

_____

_____

_____

2. Rahab and Ruth were not even members of the Jewish race. Why do you think Matthew chose to include these non-Jews (or "Gentiles") in his genealogy of Jesus?

_____

_____

_____

_____

_____

_____

_____

Joseph Accepts Jesus as His Son (Matthew 1:18–25)

18 Now the birth of Jesus Christ was as follows: After His mother Mary was betrothed to Joseph, before they came together, she was found with child of the Holy Spirit. 19 Then Joseph her husband, being a just man, and not wanting to make her a public example, was minded to put her away secretly. 20 But while he thought about these things, behold, an angel of the Lord appeared to him in a dream, saying, "Joseph, son of David, do not be afraid to take to you Mary your wife, for that which is conceived in her is of the Holy Spirit. 21 And she will bring forth a Son, and you shall call His name Jesus, for He will save His people from their sins."

22 So all this was done that it might be fulfilled which was spoken by the Lord through the prophet, saying: 23 "Behold, the virgin shall be with child, and bear a Son, and they shall call His name Immanuel," which is translated, "God with us."

24 Then Joseph, being aroused from sleep, did as the angel of the Lord commanded him and took to him his wife, 25 and did not know her till she had brought forth her firstborn Son. And he called His name Jesus.

3. This passage comprises much of Joseph's biographical information that we have available to us in the New Testament. Based on these eight verses, what conclusions can you draw about Jesus' earthly father?

_____

_____

_____

_____

_____

_____

4. Read Leviticus 20:10. Why was Mary's pregnancy especially difficult for someone who followed the Law of Moses, as Joseph did?

_____

_____

_____

_____

_____

Wise Men from the East (Matthew 2:1–12)

¹ Now after Jesus was born in Bethlehem of Judea in the days of Herod the king, behold, wise men from the East came to Jerusalem, ² saying, "Where is He who has been born King of the Jews? For we have seen His star in the East and have come to worship Him."

³ When Herod the king heard this, he was troubled, and all Jerusalem with him. ⁴ And when he had gathered all the chief priests and scribes of the people together, he inquired of them where the Christ was to be born.

⁵ So they said to him, "In Bethlehem of Judea, for thus it is written by the prophet:

⁶ 'But you, Bethlehem, in the land of Judah,
Are not the least among the rulers of Judah;
For out of you shall come a Ruler
Who will shepherd My people Israel.' "

⁷ Then Herod, when he had secretly called the wise men, determined from them what time the star appeared. ⁸ And he sent them to Bethlehem and said, "Go and search carefully for the young Child, and when you have found Him, bring back word to me, that I may come and worship Him also."

⁹ When they heard the king, they departed; and behold, the star which they had seen in the East went before them, till it came and stood over where the young Child was. ¹⁰ When they saw the star, they rejoiced with exceedingly great joy. ¹¹ And when they had come into the house, they saw the young Child with Mary His mother, and fell down and worshiped Him. And when they had opened their treasures, they presented gifts to Him: gold, frankincense, and myrrh.

¹² Then, being divinely warned in a dream that they should not return to Herod, they departed for their own country another way.

---

5. The "wise men from the East" were likely a class of astrologers from the Parthian Empire whose duties included electing the king. How did these men, sometimes referred to as "Magi," respond to meeting the child Jesus (see verses 11–12)?

_____

_____

_____

_____

_____

_____

_____

6. Traditional Christmas manger scenes place the wise men at the site of Jesus' birth, along with the shepherds, various animals, and an angel. What clues do you see in verses 9–11 that suggest the wise men may have come later?

_____

_____

_____

_____

_____

_____

The Escape to Egypt (Matthew 2:13–23)

¹³ Now when they had departed, behold, an angel of the Lord appeared to Joseph in a dream, saying, "Arise, take the young Child and His mother, flee to Egypt, and stay there until I bring you word; for Herod will seek the young Child to destroy Him."

¹⁴ When he arose, he took the young Child and His mother by night and departed for Egypt, ¹⁵ and was there until the death of Herod, that it might be fulfilled which was spoken by the Lord through the prophet, saying, "Out of Egypt I called My Son."

¹⁶ Then Herod, when he saw that he was deceived by the wise men, was exceedingly angry; and he sent forth and put to death all the male children who were in Bethlehem and in all its districts, from two years old and under, according to the time which he had determined from the wise men. ¹⁷ Then was fulfilled what was spoken by Jeremiah the prophet, saying:

¹⁸ "A voice was heard in Ramah,
Lamentation, weeping, and great mourning,
Rachel weeping for her children,
Refusing to be comforted,
Because they are no more."

¹⁹ Now when Herod was dead, behold, an angel of the Lord appeared in a dream to Joseph in Egypt, ²⁰ saying, "Arise, take the young Child and His mother, and go to the land of Israel, for those who sought the young Child's life are dead." ²¹ Then he arose, took the young Child and His mother, and came into the land of Israel.

²² But when he heard that Archelaus was reigning over Judea instead of his father Herod, he was afraid to go there. And being warned by God in a dream, he turned aside into the region of Galilee. ²³ And he came and dwelt in a city called Nazareth, that it might be fulfilled which was spoken by the prophets, "He shall be called a Nazarene."

---

7. The Bible says Satan is "the ruler of this world" (John 12:31) and holds significant influence over the earth. Jesus' arrival on the earth posed a real threat to Satan's power. Where do you see evidence in this passage of Satan trying to stop Jesus?

_____

_____

_____

_____

_____

8. Nazareth was something of a laughingstock in first-century Israel. How did Joseph's decision to settle there fulfill the Old Testament prophecy concerning the Messiah in Isaiah 53:3?

_____

_____

_____

_____

_____

REVIEWING THE STORY

Perhaps the only aspect of the Messiah's coming that conformed to Jewish expectations was His genealogy. Matthew established Jesus' royal lineage in the first chapter of his Gospel. Beyond that, virtually everything about Jesus' coming was unexpected. He was born to an unmarried girl who was betrothed to an unremarkable carpenter from the lowly town of Nazareth. His arrival did not usher in an era of political sovereignty for Israel, as expected; instead, it sparked a humanitarian atrocity. Through it all, though, God made His plan known to those involved, in memorable and often supernatural ways.

9. Isaiah had prophesied the Messiah would come "from the stem of Jesse" (11:1), who was the father of King David. Given this, why was it important for Matthew to provide a detailed genealogy of Jesus' ancestors (see Matthew 1:2–16)?

_____

_____

_____

_____

_____

10. What two names does Matthew give to describe the Messiah (see 1:21–23)? What does each name mean?

_____

_____

_____

_____

_____

11. To what extreme lengths did the power-hungry Herod go to rid himself of the newborn king (see Matthew 2:3–4, 7–8, 16)? Why do you think he reacted in this way?

_____

_____

_____

_____

_____

12. How many times do angels appear in Matthew 1–2? Why do you think God used so many angelic visits and dreams to guide Joseph and Mary during the first few years of Jesus' life?

_____

_____

_____

_____

_____

APPLYING THE MESSAGE

13. God worked through the political maneuverings of emperors and kings, including Caesar Augustus's taxation plan and King Herod's decree to kill all male babies, to fulfill prophecies made centuries earlier. What does that tell you about God's ability to work through the difficult situations in your life?

_____

_____

_____

_____

_____

14. The wise men offered Jesus gifts of gold, frankincense, and myrrh. What gifts do you have to offer Jesus? How can you present your gifts to Him or use them for His glory?

_____

_____

_____

_____

_____

REFLECTING ON THE MEANING

Christmas illustrations and decorations depicting the "holy family"—Jesus, Mary, and Joseph—inevitably show them in a serene pose, with the parents gazing lovingly at their beatific newborn. What gets lost in the celebration of Advent is the reality that Jesus, Mary, and Joseph were all profoundly outside their comfort zones.

Jesus' comfort zone (if the Son of God can be said to have a "comfort zone") was heaven, where He enjoyed the worship and adoration of the angels. He willingly gave up His heavenly glory, not to mention the independent use of His divine power and attributes, to take on human flesh. He became a helpless baby. He made Himself susceptible to pain, ridicule, betrayal, and temptation.

Mary was a humble young woman whose only expectations were to marry Joseph and raise a family. She likely never thought of herself as someone who would be visited by an angel, let alone as someone who would be chosen to give birth to the Messiah. Centuries' worth of prophecies would be fulfilled through _her_.

Joseph found himself in a near-impossible position. He was an honorable man betrothed to a pregnant woman whose child was not his own. The truth of the matter likely didn't offer him much comfort. He was betrothed to the mother of the Messiah. Joseph, a simple carpenter from Nazareth, would be responsible for raising the Son of God.

None of these people were where they *wanted* to be. But all of them were where they *needed* to be. Sometimes, God will take you beyond your comfort zone for a specific purpose. Other times, He will leave the decision to you. So, if you're given an opportunity to step beyond your comfort zone, take it. Volunteer. Teach. Share. Sacrifice. Inquire. Dare.

JOURNALING YOUR RESPONSE

What might happen if you began to venture beyond your spiritual comfort zone?

THE START OF SOMETHING BIG

Matthew 3:1–4:25

GETTING STARTED

If you had lived in Israel during the first century, how do you think you would have reacted to a man who was calling people to repent because the kingdom of heaven was near? Explain.

_____

_____

_____

_____

_____

_____

_____

_____

_____

_____

_____

_____

_____

_____

_____

_____

_____

SETTING THE STAGE

By the end of Matthew 2, Jesus is a child newly arrived in Nazareth, the town in which He would grow up. When Matthew 3 begins, Jesus is an adult, probably in His early thirties. No mention is made in Matthew's Gospel of the time jump in the narrative. One day, Jesus simply shows up at the Jordan River, where John the Baptist is ministering.

In Matthew 3–4, Jesus lays the groundwork for His public ministry: a three-year sojourn that would change the world. In His preparation, we find an example for all who would follow Him and join Him in his work. The first thing Jesus does is secure His Father's blessing. He requests John to baptize Him as a sign that He is "the Lamb of God who takes away the sin of the world" (John 1:29). As soon as Jesus emerges from the water, a voice from heaven declares, "This is My beloved Son, in whom I am well pleased" (Matthew 3:17). The heavenly Father makes it known that Jesus is doing *His* will—and that's all the affirmation Jesus needs.

After Jesus' baptism, the Holy Spirit leads Him to the wilderness, where He is tested. Satan tempts Him with the lust of the flesh, the pride of life, and the lust of the eyes. Jesus resists each temptation using the Word of God. He emerges from the encounter strong, confident, and eager to fulfill God's will.

Jesus speaks boldly the message He was sent by God to proclaim. He calls people to repentance and announces the kingdom of heaven is near. He handpicks His companions, surrounding Himself with people who are willing to sacrifice their comfort, security, status, and safety for something greater than themselves.

EXPLORING THE TEXT

John the Baptist Prepares the Way (Matthew 3:1–17)

¹ In those days John the Baptist came preaching in the wilderness of Judea, ² and saying, "Repent, for the kingdom of heaven is at hand!"
³ For this is he who was spoken of by the prophet Isaiah, saying:

"The voice of one crying in the wilderness:

'Prepare the way of the LORD;

Make His paths straight.' "

4 Now John himself was clothed in camel's hair, with a leather belt around his waist; and his food was locusts and wild honey. 5 Then Jerusalem, all Judea, and all the region around the Jordan went out to him 6 and were baptized by him in the Jordan, confessing their sins.

7 But when he saw many of the Pharisees and Sadducees coming to his baptism, he said to them, "Brood of vipers! Who warned you to flee from the wrath to come? 8 Therefore bear fruits worthy of repentance, 9 and do not think to say to yourselves, 'We have Abraham as our father.' For I say to you that God is able to raise up children to Abraham from these stones. 10 And even now the ax is laid to the root of the trees. Therefore every tree which does not bear good fruit is cut down and thrown into the fire. 11 I indeed baptize you with water unto repentance, but He who is coming after me is mightier than I, whose sandals I am not worthy to carry. He will baptize you with the Holy Spirit and fire. 12 His winnowing fan is in His hand, and He will thoroughly clean out His threshing floor, and gather His wheat into the barn; but He will burn up the chaff with unquenchable fire."

13 Then Jesus came from Galilee to John at the Jordan to be baptized by him. 14 And John tried to prevent Him, saying, "I need to be baptized by You, and are You coming to me?"

15 But Jesus answered and said to him, "Permit it to be so now, for thus it is fitting for us to fulfill all righteousness." Then he allowed Him.

16 When He had been baptized, Jesus came up immediately from the water; and behold, the heavens were opened to Him, and He saw the Spirit of God descending like a dove and alighting upon Him. 17 And suddenly a voice came from heaven, saying, "This is My beloved Son, in whom I am well pleased."

1. John had pointed words for the Pharisees and Sadducees, the religious leaders of Israel (see verses 7–12). Why was John so tough on these leaders?

_____

_____

_____

_____

_____

_____

2. What was John's first reaction when Jesus asked to be baptized (see verse 13)? Why do you think John responded this way?

_____

_____

_____

_____

_____

_____

Jesus Is Tested in the Wilderness (Matthew 4:1–11)

¹ Then Jesus was led up by the Spirit into the wilderness to be tempted by the devil. ² And when He had fasted forty days and forty nights, afterward He was hungry. ³ Now when the tempter came to Him, he said, "If You are the Son of God, command that these stones become bread."

⁴ But He answered and said, "It is written, 'Man shall not live by bread alone, but by every word that proceeds from the mouth of God.' "

⁵ Then the devil took Him up into the holy city, set Him on the pinnacle of the temple, ⁶ and said to Him, "If You are the Son of God, throw Yourself down. For it is written:

'He shall give His angels charge over you,'

and,

'In their hands they shall bear you up,
Lest you dash your foot against a stone.' "

⁷ Jesus said to him, "It is written again, 'You shall not tempt the LORD your God.' "

⁸ Again, the devil took Him up on an exceedingly high mountain, and showed Him all the kingdoms of the world and their glory. ⁹ And he said to Him, "All these things I will give You if You will fall down and worship me."

¹⁰ Then Jesus said to him, "Away with you, Satan! For it is written, 'You shall worship the Lord your God, and Him only you shall serve.' "

¹¹ Then the devil left Him, and behold, angels came and ministered to Him.

---

3. What are each of the ways that Satan tempted Jesus (see verses 3, 5–6, 8–9)?

_____

_____

_____

_____

_____

_____

_____

_____

_____

_____

_____

_____

4. What do Jesus' three responses to Satan all have in common (see verses 4, 7, 10)?

_____

_____

_____

_____

Jesus Begins to Preach (Matthew 4:12–17)

[12] Now when Jesus heard that John had been put in prison, He departed to Galilee. [13] And leaving Nazareth, He came and dwelt in Capernaum, which is by the sea, in the regions of Zebulun and Naphtali, [14] that it might be fulfilled which was spoken by Isaiah the prophet, saying:

[15] "The land of Zebulun and the land of Naphtali,
By the way of the sea, beyond the Jordan,
Galilee of the Gentiles:

[16] The people who sat in darkness have seen a great light,
And upon those who sat in the region and shadow of death
Light has dawned."

[17] From that time Jesus began to preach and to say, "Repent, for the kingdom of heaven is at hand."

5. Galilee was a backwater region. Unlike Jerusalem, it was filled with many non-religious types. Why did Jesus move His base of operations there (see verses 14–16)?

_____

_____

_____

6. What was the main focus of Jesus' message (see verse 17)?

_____

_____

_____

_____

_____

_____

_____

_____

_____

_____

Jesus Calls His First Disciples (Matthew 4:18–25)

¹⁸ And Jesus, walking by the Sea of Galilee, saw two brothers, Simon called Peter, and Andrew his brother, casting a net into the sea; for they were fishermen. ¹⁹ Then He said to them, "Follow Me, and I will make you fishers of men." ²⁰ They immediately left their nets and followed Him.

²¹ Going on from there, He saw two other brothers, James the son of Zebedee, and John his brother, in the boat with Zebedee their father, mending their nets. He called them, ²² and immediately they left the boat and their father, and followed Him.

²³ And Jesus went about all Galilee, teaching in their synagogues, preaching the gospel of the kingdom, and healing all kinds of sickness and all kinds of disease among the people. ²⁴ Then His fame went throughout all Syria; and they brought to Him all sick people who were afflicted with various diseases and torments, and those who were demon-possessed, epileptics, and paralytics; and He healed them. ²⁵ Great multitudes followed Him—from Galilee, and from Decapolis, Jerusalem, Judea, and beyond the Jordan.

7. Jesus' first disciples were blue-collar workers who were a bit rough around the edges. He could have chosen people who were more educated, socially acceptable, and "religious." What do you think Jesus saw in men like Simon Peter, Andrew, James, and John?

_____

_____

_____

_____

_____

_____

8. What do you think Simon Peter, Andrew, James, and John saw in Jesus that made them drop everything in order to follow Him?

_____

_____

_____

_____

_____

_____

REVIEWING THE STORY

Matthew 3–4 offers a glimpse of Jesus before the masses became aware of Him. John the Baptist had an inkling of what Jesus' arrival meant. So did Satan, who jumped at the opportunity to put Jesus to the test. Although the fullness of Jesus' mission was not yet apparent, His commitment to his heavenly Father, His masterful strategy for defeating Satan, His choice of companions, and His compassion for those who were hurting were all in full view. The world had changed forever . . . though few people realized it at the time.

9. Look at John the Baptist's reaction to Jesus' request to be baptized (see Matthew 3:14–15). He is both humble ("I need to be baptized by you") and obedient ("Then he allowed Him"). Why are those two qualities so important?

_____

_____

_____

_____

_____

_____

_____

10. What was Jesus' primary strategy for countering Satan's temptations (see Matthew 4:1–10)? Why was it so effective?

_____

_____

_____

_____

_____

_____

_____

_____

_____

11. Psalm 32:5 and Isaiah 55:7 offer insights into what it means to repent. Why do you think repentance was the central theme of Jesus' message?

_____

_____

_____

_____

_____

_____

12. Jesus' healing ministry could have threatened to overshadow His message. What are some things that tend to overshadow Jesus' message in our culture today?

_____

_____

_____

_____

_____

_____

APPLYING THE MESSAGE

13. Jesus heard God's affirming voice immediately after His baptism. How do you know when God is pleased with you?

_____

_____

_____

_____

_____

_____

14. What do you have in common with people like John the Baptist, Peter, Andrew, James, and John? What does Jesus see in you? What might He accomplish through you?

_____

_____

_____

_____

_____

_____

_____

_____

REFLECTING ON THE MEANING

"Then Jesus was led up by the Spirit into the wilderness to be tempted by the devil" (Matthew 4:1). The Greek word for _temptation_ is often translated as _trial, test,_ or _prove_. God doesn't tempt us directly to do evil (see James 1:12), but He does put us through trials. He puts us in the furnace. He puts us in the lions' den.

When Jesus was tempted by the devil, it was the Spirit who led Him there, and for good reason. Positive things can come from temptation or testing. For one thing, temptation reveals what is in a person's heart. Abraham was tested when God instructed him to sacrifice his son Isaac (see Genesis 22). Abraham was tempted to grab his son and run, yet he resisted the temptation. He obeyed God's command—and breathed a huge sigh of relief when an angel of the Lord stopped him from sacrificing Isaac.

Before that trial, Abraham knew he loved God in _theory_. Afterward, he knew he loved God in _fact_. He had taken that which was most precious to him and offered it to God.

God can also use temptation to reinforce a person's will. Every time you face temptation and resist it, it is like digging a deeper groove into your spirit—one that gives you leverage the next time temptation comes around. The more often you resist, the more leverage you get.

Finally, God can use temptation to remind others around you of His grace and goodness. When people see you resist temptation—when they see God at work in your life—it gives them hope. It gives them encouragement. And it gives them a template to follow.

The power to impact someone else's walk with Christ is an extraordinary gift and an extraordinary responsibility. You can embrace it by being transparent about the temptations you face and the prayerful strategies you use to resist them.

JOURNALING YOUR RESPONSE

Whose spiritual example has inspired or encouraged you? Who might look to you for inspiration or encouragement?

THE SERMON ON THE MOUNT

Matthew 5:1–7:29

GETTING STARTED

What are some things you thought would bring you happiness . . . but didn't?

_____

_____

_____

_____

_____

_____

_____

_____

_____

_____

_____

SETTING THE STAGE

In Matthew 5, Jesus begins to deliver a teaching that is today called the "Sermon on the Mount." He starts by revealing to His followers the secrets of true happiness (or blessedness), which are known as the "Beatitudes." His approach to happiness is radical, to say the least.

Jesus sets the tone for His message in His very first words: "Blessed are the poor in spirit" (verse 3). Those who are poor in spirit recognize they are out of step with the world. If you live according to the Beatitudes, you will find yourself in conflict with everything that is going on around you. You will feel the tension at the very core of who you are.

The poor in spirit are those who don't boast about their talents or achievements because they know they have nothing they didn't receive from God. If they are gifted, it's because they have been given much. Having a poverty of spirit means having a proper assessment of who you are inwardly without God.

Those who are poor in spirit also reach out to others with a spirit of love and compassion. They find their highest joy in serving others for the kingdom of God. Being poor in spirit means putting the needs of others ahead of your own.

In Matthew 6, Jesus goes on to teach His disciples to pray that God's will "be done on earth as it is in heaven" (verse 10). Jesus is talking about God's will being done in the lives of His followers. As you embrace the kingdom of God in your life, the kingdom lives within you, and you become a part of it. When that happens, you discover the kind of happiness the world will never be able to manufacture or even understand.

There is no happiness like knowing, in the core of your being, that you are *in the center of God's will, doing what God wants you to do, and loving every minute of it!*

Exploring the Text

The Beatitudes (Matthew 5:1–12)

¹ And seeing the multitudes, He went up on a mountain, and when He was seated His disciples came to Him. ² Then He opened His mouth and taught them, saying:

³ "Blessed are the poor in spirit,
For theirs is the kingdom of heaven.

4 Blessed are those who mourn,
For they shall be comforted.
5 Blessed are the meek,
For they shall inherit the earth.
6 Blessed are those who hunger and thirst for righteousness,
For they shall be filled.
7 Blessed are the merciful,
For they shall obtain mercy.
8 Blessed are the pure in heart,
For they shall see God.
9 Blessed are the peacemakers,
For they shall be called sons of God.
10 Blessed are those who are persecuted for righteousness' sake,
For theirs is the kingdom of heaven.

11 Blessed are you when they revile and persecute you, and say all kinds of evil against you falsely for My sake. 12 Rejoice and be exceedingly glad, for great is your reward in heaven, for so they persecuted the prophets who were before you."

---

1. "Those who mourn" (verse 4) are those who are moved to sorrow by their own sin and those who feel the sorrow of others. How does feeling such godly sorrow lead to blessing?

_____

_____

_____

_____

_____

_____

_____

_____

2. Peacemakers have two roles: (1) to bring God and people together, and (2) to bring people and people together. Why are both of these roles essential?

_____

_____

_____

_____

_____

_____

_____

Salt and Light (Matthew 5:13–20)

13 "You are the salt of the earth; but if the salt loses its flavor, how shall it be seasoned? It is then good for nothing but to be thrown out and trampled underfoot by men.

14 "You are the light of the world. A city that is set on a hill cannot be hidden.15 Nor do they light a lamp and put it under a basket, but on a lampstand, and it gives light to all who are in the house. 16 Let your light so shine before men, that they may see your good works and glorify your Father in heaven.

17 "Do not think that I came to destroy the Law or the Prophets. I did not come to destroy but to fulfill. 18 For assuredly, I say to you, till heaven and earth pass away, one jot or one tittle will by no means pass from the law till all is fulfilled. 19 Whoever therefore breaks one of the least of these commandments, and teaches men so, shall be called least in the kingdom of heaven; but whoever does and teaches them, he shall be called great in the kingdom of heaven. 20 For I say to you, that unless your righteousness exceeds the righteousness of the scribes and Pharisees, you will by no means enter the kingdom of heaven."

3. If you follow Christ, you are "the salt of the earth" and "the light of the world" (verses 13–14). Do you see this more as an opportunity or a challenge? Explain.

_____

_____

_____

_____

_____

4. What do you think Jesus meant when He said that He did not come "to destroy the Law or the Prophets" (verse 17)? What standard did He set for His followers?

_____

_____

_____

_____

_____

_____

Teaching on Prayer (Matthew 6:5–15)

⁵ "And when you pray, you shall not be like the hypocrites. For they love to pray standing in the synagogues and on the corners of the streets, that they may be seen by men. Assuredly, I say to you, they have their reward. ⁶ But you, when you pray, go into your room, and when you have shut your door, pray to your Father who is in the secret place; and your Father who sees in secret will reward you openly. ⁷ And when you pray, do not use vain repetitions as the heathen do. For they think that they will be heard for their many words.

⁸ "Therefore do not be like them. For your Father knows the things you have need of before you ask Him. ⁹ In this manner, therefore, pray:

Our Father in heaven,

Hallowed be Your name.

¹⁰ Your kingdom come.

Your will be done

On earth as it is in heaven.

¹¹ Give us this day our daily bread.

¹² And forgive us our debts,

As we forgive our debtors.

¹³ And do not lead us into temptation,

But deliver us from the evil one.

For Yours is the kingdom and the power and the glory forever.

Amen.

¹⁴ "For if you forgive men their trespasses, your heavenly Father will also forgive you. ¹⁵ But if you do not forgive men their trespasses, neither will your Father forgive your trespasses."

---

5. Praying "like the hypocrites" (verse 5) means calling attention to yourself when you pray. Praying like "the heathen" (verse 7) means mindlessly repeating certain words and phrases. What is the best strategy for avoiding these two types of mistakes in prayer?

6. Praying, "Give us this day our daily bread" (verse 11), encourages us to depend on God for our needs. It also encourages a daily discipline of prayer and eliminates the need for worry. Why is it so difficult to take this kind of day-by-day approach to our needs?

_____

_____

_____

Bearing Good Fruit (Matthew 7:15–27)

15 "Beware of false prophets, who come to you in sheep's clothing, but inwardly they are ravenous wolves. 16 You will know them by their fruits. Do men gather grapes from thornbushes or figs from thistles? 17 Even so, every good tree bears good fruit, but a bad tree bears bad fruit. 18 A good tree cannot bear bad fruit, nor can a bad tree bear good fruit. 19 Every tree that does not bear good fruit is cut down and thrown into the fire. 20 Therefore by their fruits you will know them.

21 "Not everyone who says to Me, 'Lord, Lord,' shall enter the kingdom of heaven, but he who does the will of My Father in heaven. 22 Many will say to Me in that day, 'Lord, Lord, have we not prophesied in Your name, cast out demons in Your name, and done many wonders in Your name?' 23 And then I will declare to them, 'I never knew you; depart from Me, you who practice lawlessness!'

24 "Therefore whoever hears these sayings of Mine, and does them, I will liken him to a wise man who built his house on the rock: 25 and the rain descended, the floods came, and the winds blew and beat on that house; and it did not fall, for it was founded on the rock.

26 "But everyone who hears these sayings of Mine, and does not do them, will be like a foolish man who built his house on the sand: 27 and the rain descended, the floods came, and the winds blew and beat on that house; and it fell. And great was its fall."

7. Genuine spiritual fruit involves character (who you are), conduct (what you do), contributions (what you give), communication (what you say), and converts (who you win for Christ). What are some "bad fruits" by which people can recognize false prophets?

_____

_____

_____

_____

_____

8. In what ways are those who listen to Jesus' teachings and apply those teachings to their lives like the man who built his house on the rock (see verses 24–25)?

_____

_____

_____

_____

_____

REVIEWING THE STORY

In Matthew 5–7, Jesus condensed the Christian faith to its most essential elements. In one epic sermon, He identified the select groups of people—including the poor in spirit, the meek, the merciful, the pure in heart, and the peacemakers—who will experience genuine happiness and fulfillment. He helped His followers recognize the difference we each can make in the world. He revealed the limitations of the Law of Moses. He showed us how to pray effectively. He taught us how to identify false teachers. He showed us what our priorities should be.

9. Mercy is love that is given when it is not deserved. It is forgiveness that is given when it is not earned. What did Jesus say would happen to those who extended mercy to others (see Matthew 5:7)? Why did Jesus place such a high priority on showing mercy to others?

_____

_____

_____

_____

_____

_____

10. What are some ways that Jesus calls His followers to represent Him to the world? What does it mean to be a light that is "set on a hill" (Matthew 5:14)?

_____

_____

_____

_____

_____

_____

11. Why do you think Jesus began and ended the Lord's Prayer with praise (see Matthew 6:9, 13)?

_____

_____

_____

_____

_____

_____

12. What does Jesus say about bearing good fruit for Him (see Matthew 7:15–23)? What is the problem with just listening to what Jesus says but not acting on His words?

_____

_____

_____

_____

_____

_____

_____

_____

_____

APPLYING THE MESSAGE

13. The Lord's Prayer is the most famous prayer in the world. In just sixty-six words, Jesus taught His disciples how to pray. What are some ways you can use the Lord's Prayer to help you pray more consistently and purposefully?

_____

_____

_____

_____

_____

_____

_____

_____

_____

14. What type of "good fruits" or positive behaviors would you like others to see in you? How can you make those behaviors happen?

_____

_____

_____

_____

_____

REFLECTING ON THE MEANING

The Declaration of Independence of the United States identifies three "unalienable rights" that are endowed to people by their Creator: life, liberty, and the pursuit of happiness. The quest for happiness is hardwired into the American psyche, and that quest takes many different forms. One person buys a dozen homes to be happy, while another goes into the wilderness to live as a hermit. One person finds happiness in working out, while another tries to find it by using mind-altering drugs. One couple thinks happiness is children, so they have eight of them. Another couple is convinced children would get in the way of happiness, so they go childless.

Everyone who seeks happiness finds it with varying degrees of success. But almost everyone discovers the things he or she _thought_ would bring happiness didn't pan out. Jesus understood the frustration and desperation that come when our quest for happiness is thwarted. So, in his Sermon on the Mount, He reveals three eternal truths about happiness.

First, true happiness _is part of God's purpose for us_. In John 10:10, Jesus says, "I have come that they may have life, and that they may have it more abundantly." He clashed with the dour religious leaders of the day and enjoyed the company of people who knew how to have a good time. He took great delight in the simple pleasures of life.

Second, the pursuit of true happiness _is a journey inward_. Look at the people Jesus identifies as "blessed" in the Beatitudes: the poor, the hungry and thirsty, the persecuted, and the sorrowful. Their exterior circumstances have nothing to do with their happiness. Their joy comes from within.

Third, true happiness *is a byproduct, not a goal*. If you pursue God's will, use the gifts He provides to you, and seek ways to make other people's lives better, you will find this leads to you experiencing genuine happiness.

JOURNALING YOUR RESPONSE

What steps can you take today to become a happier, or more blessed, person?

LESSON *four*

WHO IS THIS MAN?

Matthew 8:1–9:38

GETTING STARTED

How would you respond to someone who thought Jesus was nothing more than an ancient philosopher or a good teacher?

_____

_____

_____

_____

_____

_____

_____

_____

_____

_____

_____

_____

_____

_____

_____

_____

_____

_____

_____

SETTING THE STAGE

From the very beginning of His ministry, Jesus had a reputation as an extraordinary teacher. His Sermon on the Mount shook the spiritual foundations of His followers and called them to radically realign their priorities. Jesus showed He was a compassionate healer as well, curing people of seizures, paralysis, demon possession, and all manner of sickness and pain.

As Jesus' ministry gained momentum, people began to see Him as more than just an itinerant preacher or healer. You can sense it in the awestruck but reverent words of the leper who approached Him and said, "Lord, if You are willing, You can make me clean" (Matthew 8:2). The people Jesus healed spread the news about Him—despite His instruction not to share their story. As Jesus' fame grew, so did His aura of gravitas and importance. A Roman centurion was so convinced of Jesus' authority, and his own unworthiness to have Jesus in his house, that he stated Jesus could heal his sick servant by merely speaking the word. Even demons recognized Him on sight as the Son of God!

One time, when Jesus and His disciples were caught in a furious storm at sea, He calmed the winds and the waves with a single command. His disciples marveled at His power, saying, "Who can this be, that even the winds and the sea obey Him?" (8:27). When He later healed a demon-possessed and mute man, the astonished crowd declared, "It was never seen like this in Israel!" (9:33). Yet as astonished as the disciples and crowds were, they would have been even more amazed if they knew the full truth of Jesus' identity and calling.

EXPLORING THE TEXT

The Faith of the Leper and the Centurion (Matthew 8:1–13)

¹ When He had come down from the mountain, great multitudes followed Him. ² And behold, a leper came and worshiped Him, saying, "Lord, if You are willing, You can make me clean." ³ Then Jesus put

out His hand and touched him, saying, "I am willing; be cleansed." Immediately his leprosy was cleansed.

⁴ And Jesus said to him, "See that you tell no one; but go your way, show yourself to the priest, and offer the gift that Moses commanded, as a testimony to them."

⁵ Now when Jesus had entered Capernaum, a centurion came to Him, pleading with Him, ⁶ saying, "Lord, my servant is lying at home paralyzed, dreadfully tormented."

⁷ And Jesus said to him, "I will come and heal him."

⁸ The centurion answered and said, "Lord, I am not worthy that You should come under my roof. But only speak a word, and my servant will be healed. ⁹ For I also am a man under authority, having soldiers under me. And I say to this one, 'Go,' and he goes; and to another, 'Come,' and he comes; and to my servant, 'Do this,' and he does it."

¹⁰ When Jesus heard it, He marveled, and said to those who followed, "Assuredly, I say to you, I have not found such great faith, not even in Israel. ¹¹ And I say to you that many will come from east and west, and sit down with Abraham, Isaac, and Jacob in the kingdom of heaven. ¹² But the sons of the kingdom will be cast out into outer darkness. There will be weeping and gnashing of teeth." ¹³ Then Jesus said to the centurion, "Go your way; and as you have believed, so let it be done for you." And his servant was healed that same hour.

---

1. How did the man with leprosy express his faith that Jesus could heal him? How did Jesus respond to the man (see verses 2–4)?

2. How did the centurion express his faith that Jesus could heal his servant? What caused Jesus to marvel at the centurion's words (see verses 8–10)?

_____

_____

_____

_____

_____

Jesus' Authority (Matthew 8:23–34)

23 Now when He got into a boat, His disciples followed Him. 24 And suddenly a great tempest arose on the sea, so that the boat was covered with the waves. But He was asleep. 25 Then His disciples came to Him and awoke Him, saying, "Lord, save us! We are perishing!"

26 But He said to them, "Why are you fearful, O you of little faith?" Then He arose and rebuked the winds and the sea, and there was a great calm. 27 So the men marveled, saying, "Who can this be, that even the winds and the sea obey Him?"

28 When He had come to the other side, to the country of the Gergesenes, there met Him two demon-possessed men, coming out of the tombs, exceedingly fierce, so that no one could pass that way. 29 And suddenly they cried out, saying, "What have we to do with You, Jesus, You Son of God? Have You come here to torment us before the time?"

30 Now a good way off from them there was a herd of many swine feeding. 31 So the demons begged Him, saying, "If You cast us out, permit us to go away into the herd of swine."

32 And He said to them, "Go." So when they had come out, they went into the herd of swine. And suddenly the whole herd of swine ran violently down the steep place into the sea, and perished in the water.

33 Then those who kept them fled; and they went away into the city and told everything, including what had happened to the

demon-possessed men. ³⁴ And behold, the whole city came out to meet Jesus. And when they saw Him, they begged Him to depart from their region.

3. Why do you think the disciples panicked in the storm (see verses 24–25), even though they had seen Jesus perform other miracles?

_____

_____

_____

_____

_____

_____

_____

_____

4. How did Jesus demonstrate His authority when healing the demon-possessed men? Why do you think the people of the city reacted the way they did to Jesus after the healing (see verses 30–34)?

_____

_____

_____

_____

_____

_____

_____

_____

_____

Jesus Calls the Sinners to Repentance (Matthew 9:9–13)

⁹ As Jesus passed on from there, He saw a man named Matthew sitting at the tax office. And He said to him, "Follow Me." So he arose and followed Him.

¹⁰ Now it happened, as Jesus sat at the table in the house, that behold, many tax collectors and sinners came and sat down with Him and His disciples. ¹¹ And when the Pharisees saw it, they said to His disciples, "Why does your Teacher eat with tax collectors and sinners?"

¹² When Jesus heard that, He said to them, "Those who are well have no need of a physician, but those who are sick. ¹³ But go and learn what this means: 'I desire mercy and not sacrifice.' For I did not come to call the righteous, but sinners, to repentance."

5. What was Jesus communicating about God's character and priorities when He told the Pharisees, "I desire mercy and not sacrifice" (verse 13)?

_____

_____

_____

_____

_____

6. How did Jesus' understanding of God's character influence His ministry? To whom did Jesus choose to reach out and minister?

_____

_____

_____

_____

_____

The Compassion of Jesus (Matthew 9:27–38)

[27] When Jesus departed from there, two blind men followed Him, crying out and saying, "Son of David, have mercy on us!"

[28] And when He had come into the house, the blind men came to Him. And Jesus said to them, "Do you believe that I am able to do this?"

They said to Him, "Yes, Lord."

[29] Then He touched their eyes, saying, "According to your faith let it be to you." [30] And their eyes were opened. And Jesus sternly warned them, saying, "See that no one knows it." [31] But when they had departed, they spread the news about Him in all that country.

[32] As they went out, behold, they brought to Him a man, mute and demon-possessed. [33] And when the demon was cast out, the mute spoke. And the multitudes marveled, saying, "It was never seen like this in Israel!"

[34] But the Pharisees said, "He casts out demons by the ruler of the demons."

[35] Then Jesus went about all the cities and villages, teaching in their synagogues, preaching the gospel of the kingdom, and healing every sickness and every disease among the people. [36] But when He saw the multitudes, He was moved with compassion for them, because they were weary and scattered, like sheep having no shepherd. [37] Then He said to His disciples, "The harvest truly is plentiful, but the laborers are few. [38] Therefore pray the Lord of the harvest to send out laborers into His harvest."

---

7. Why do you think Jesus asked the blind men if they *believed* He could heal them before He performed the miracle?

_____

_____

_____

_____

8. What was Jesus' ministry strategy? What motivated Him to minister to others (see verses 36–37)?

_____

_____

_____

_____

_____

_____

_____

_____

REVIEWING THE STORY

Jesus' power and authority are on full display in Matthew 8–9. The man with leprosy recognized it. The Roman centurion recognized it. The disciples recognized it when Jesus stopped a storm at sea in its tracks. Friends of the paralyzed man recognized it. So did the people who saw Jesus raise a young woman from the dead—as well as the woman who had been suffering from a blood disorder for twelve years. In fact, the only ones who _didn't_ recognize Jesus' power and authority were the Pharisees.

9. Why was the centurion's humility so important to the story of Jesus healing his servant (see Matthew 8:5–13)?

_____

_____

_____

_____

_____

_____

_____

10. How does the disciples' reaction to Jesus calming the storm indicate a shift in how they viewed Him (see Matthew 8:26–27)? What had they recognized about Jesus in that moment?

_____

_____

_____

_____

_____

_____

11. How did Jesus respond when the Pharisees accused Him of eating with "tax collectors and sinners" (Matthew 9:11)? What does this say about Jesus' mission?

_____

_____

_____

_____

_____

_____

12. Why do you think the people Jesus healed continued to ignore His instructions not to tell anyone about how it happened (see Matthew 9:31)? What impact do you think that had on Jesus' ministry?

_____

_____

_____

_____

_____

_____

APPLYING THE MESSAGE

13. When have you experienced "storms" in your life that made you panic? What did you do? How did Jesus calm those storms?

_____

_____

_____

_____

_____

_____

_____

_____

_____

_____

14. When Jesus passed by Matthew, He offered an invitation to follow Him. What would it look like for you to reach out to your friends and invite them to follow Christ?

_____

_____

_____

_____

_____

_____

_____

_____

_____

REFLECTING ON THE MEANING

The Pharisees weren't quite as obtuse or dense as they seemed. They recognized Jesus as a teacher unlike any other *and* as a formidable opponent. However, they had to dismiss Him as a heretic, blasphemer, or worse because He represented a seismic disruption to Israel's spiritual status quo.

The Pharisees and other religious leaders had too much invested in the present state of affairs to let an upstart rabbi from Nazareth ruin it. They had dedicated their lives to studying Moses' Law, and their knowledge gave them power, authority, and prestige. If Jesus really was the Messiah, it meant their understanding of God was incorrect. To acknowledge Jesus would cost them their prestige, pride, and standing in the community.

We face a similar dilemma today. Jesus' actions force us to make a choice: dismiss Him (like the Pharisees did) as a good teacher or a noteworthy spiritual philosopher, or embrace Him (like the centurion did) as the Son of God. Each decision comes with its own set of consequences. If we dismiss Jesus, we preserve our pride and spiritual status quo . . . but at great cost. We enjoy temporary status and pleasure but are cut off from God's power and plan.

However, embracing Jesus as God comes with its own ramifications. When we embrace Christ, He upsets and demolishes our own pride, power, and authority. Socially, we open ourselves to accusations of being naïve, foolish, narrow-minded, out of touch, and intolerant. We run the risk of losing people's respect, being excluded from certain social settings, and becoming a target of attacks from those who have dismissed and rejected Jesus. Yet, when we embrace Jesus, we experience the abundant life God originally created us to enjoy.

The decision we make hangs on how we answer a single simple question: "Is Jesus who He says He is?" The choice—and the consequences—are ours to claim.

JOURNALING YOUR RESPONSE

In Matthew 9:9, the author tells the story of his decision to embrace Jesus. If you had one verse to tell the story of *your* decision to follow Jesus, what would you say?

SHEEP, SNAKES, AND DOVES

Matthew 10:1–12:50

GETTING STARTED

What is the hardest job or assignment you've ever been given? What made it so difficult?

SETTING THE STAGE

Jesus' life on earth was short—just thirty-three years. His public ministry (which makes up the bulk of Matthew's Gospel) only lasted *three* years. To maximize His impact, Jesus commissioned and sent out His followers—starting with His twelve handpicked disciples—to spread His word, first to the Jewish people and then to the Gentiles. Jesus was honest. He made it clear that not everyone would listen to the disciples' message. They would face rejection—and worse. However, He encouraged them to endure rejection and persecution because the reward for their service would far outweigh whatever hardships they suffered.

As Jesus' impact increased, so did His scrutiny by the Pharisees. An itinerant rabbi with delusions of grandeur was one thing . . . but One with the power to perform miracles (and, in the process, garner broad support among the Jewish people) presented a real threat to their status and position in society. So they tried to trip Him up with loaded questions and accusations of violating their religious law. They failed. In every confrontation, Jesus turned their questions back on them and exposed their hypocrisy. He made them look foolish, which only strengthened their resolve to take more drastic measures against Him.

Jesus' message and actions not only confused the Pharisees, but they also created questions among His followers. The Jewish people had anticipated the Messiah for centuries, but no one thought He would look, sound, or act like Jesus did. Even John the Baptist, one of Jesus' staunchest allies, needed a reminder that Jesus was who He claimed to be. Jesus assured John—and all of His followers—that their faith in Him was well placed.

EXPLORING THE TEXT

Jesus Sends Out the Disciples (Matthew 10:1–20)

> ¹ And when He had called His twelve disciples to Him, He gave them power over unclean spirits, to cast them out, and to heal

all kinds of sickness and all kinds of disease. [2] Now the names of the twelve apostles are these: first, Simon, who is called Peter, and Andrew his brother; James the son of Zebedee, and John his brother; [3] Philip and Bartholomew; Thomas and Matthew the tax collector; James the son of Alphaeus, and Lebbaeus, whose surname was Thaddaeus; [4] Simon the Canaanite, and Judas Iscariot, who also betrayed Him.

[5] These twelve Jesus sent out and commanded them, saying: "Do not go into the way of the Gentiles, and do not enter a city of the Samaritans. [6] But go rather to the lost sheep of the house of Israel. [7] And as you go, preach, saying, 'The kingdom of heaven is at hand.' [8] Heal the sick, cleanse the lepers, raise the dead, cast out demons. Freely you have received, freely give. [9] Provide neither gold nor silver nor copper in your money belts, [10] nor bag for your journey, nor two tunics, nor sandals, nor staffs; for a worker is worthy of his food.

[11] "Now whatever city or town you enter, inquire who in it is worthy, and stay there till you go out. [12] And when you go into a household, greet it. [13] If the household is worthy, let your peace come upon it. But if it is not worthy, let your peace return to you. [14] And whoever will not receive you nor hear your words, when you depart from that house or city, shake off the dust from your feet. [15] Assuredly, I say to you, it will be more tolerable for the land of Sodom and Gomorrah in the day of judgment than for that city!

[16] "Behold, I send you out as sheep in the midst of wolves. Therefore be wise as serpents and harmless as doves. [17] But beware of men, for they will deliver you up to councils and scourge you in their synagogues. [18] You will be brought before governors and kings for My sake, as a testimony to them and to the Gentiles. [19] But when they deliver you up, do not worry about how or what you should speak. For it will be given to you in that hour what you should speak; [20] for it is not you who speak, but the Spirit of your Father who speaks in you."

1. What are some of the instructions Jesus gave to the twelve disciples when He sent them out (see verses 5–15)?

_____

_____

_____

_____

2. What do you think Jesus meant when He instructed His followers to "be wise as serpents and harmless as doves" (verse 16)?

_____

_____

_____

_____

John the Baptist Sends Messengers to Jesus (Matthew 11:1–15)

¹ Now it came to pass, when Jesus finished commanding His twelve disciples, that He departed from there to teach and to preach in their cities.

² And when John had heard in prison about the works of Christ, he sent two of his disciples ³ and said to Him, "Are You the Coming One, or do we look for another?"

⁴ Jesus answered and said to them, "Go and tell John the things which you hear and see: ⁵ The blind see and the lame walk; the lepers are cleansed and the deaf hear; the dead are raised up and the poor have the gospel preached to them. ⁶ And blessed is he who is not offended because of Me."

⁷ As they departed, Jesus began to say to the multitudes concerning John: "What did you go out into the wilderness to see? A reed shaken by the wind? ⁸ But what did you go out to see? A man clothed in soft garments? Indeed, those who wear soft clothing are in kings'

houses. ⁹ But what did you go out to see? A prophet? Yes, I say to you, and more than a prophet. ¹⁰ For this is he of whom it is written:

'Behold, I send My messenger before Your face,
Who will prepare Your way before You.'

¹¹ "Assuredly, I say to you, among those born of women there has not risen one greater than John the Baptist; but he who is least in the kingdom of heaven is greater than he. ¹² And from the days of John the Baptist until now the kingdom of heaven suffers violence, and the violent take it by force. ¹³ For all the prophets and the law prophesied until John. ¹⁴ And if you are willing to receive it, he is Elijah who is to come. ¹⁵ He who has ears to hear, let him hear!"

3. In light of John 1:29–34, what is surprising here about John the Baptist's question to Jesus (see Matthew 11:3)?

_____

_____

_____

_____

_____

4. How did Jesus describe John the Baptist to the people? What role did He say that John had come into the world to perform (see verses 7–10)?

_____

_____

_____

_____

_____

_____

Jesus Is Lord of the Sabbath (Matthew 12:1–14)

¹ At that time Jesus went through the grainfields on the Sabbath. And His disciples were hungry, and began to pluck heads of grain and to eat. ² And when the Pharisees saw it, they said to Him, "Look, Your disciples are doing what is not lawful to do on the Sabbath!"

³ But He said to them, "Have you not read what David did when he was hungry, he and those who were with him: ⁴ how he entered the house of God and ate the showbread which was not lawful for him to eat, nor for those who were with him, but only for the priests? ⁵ Or have you not read in the law that on the Sabbath the priests in the temple profane the Sabbath, and are blameless? ⁶ Yet I say to you that in this place there is One greater than the temple. ⁷ But if you had known what this means, 'I desire mercy and not sacrifice,' you would not have condemned the guiltless. ⁸ For the Son of Man is Lord even of the Sabbath."

⁹ Now when He had departed from there, He went into their synagogue. ¹⁰ And behold, there was a man who had a withered hand. And they asked Him, saying, "Is it lawful to heal on the Sabbath?"— that they might accuse Him.

¹¹ Then He said to them, "What man is there among you who has one sheep, and if it falls into a pit on the Sabbath, will not lay hold of it and lift it out? ¹² Of how much more value then is a man than a sheep? Therefore it is lawful to do good on the Sabbath." ¹³ Then He said to the man, "Stretch out your hand." And he stretched it out, and it was restored as whole as the other. ¹⁴ Then the Pharisees went out and plotted against Him, how they might destroy Him.

---

5. What specific charges did the Pharisees level against Jesus (see verses 1–2, 9–14)?

_____

_____

_____

6. Why do you think Jesus used a story from Scripture about David and his men eating the consecrated bread to answer the Pharisees' accusations (see verses 3–8)?

A House Divided Cannot Stand (Matthew 12:22–32)

²² Then one was brought to Him who was demon-possessed, blind and mute; and He healed him, so that the blind and mute man both spoke and saw. ²³ And all the multitudes were amazed and said, "Could this be the Son of David?"

²⁴ Now when the Pharisees heard it they said, "This fellow does not cast out demons except by Beelzebub, the ruler of the demons."

²⁵ But Jesus knew their thoughts, and said to them: "Every kingdom divided against itself is brought to desolation, and every city or house divided against itself will not stand. ²⁶ If Satan casts out Satan, he is divided against himself. How then will his kingdom stand? ²⁷ And if I cast out demons by Beelzebub, by whom do your sons cast them out? Therefore they shall be your judges. ²⁸ But if I cast out demons by the Spirit of God, surely the kingdom of God has come upon you. ²⁹ Or how can one enter a strong man's house and plunder his goods, unless he first binds the strong man? And then he will plunder his house. ³⁰ He who is not with Me is against Me, and he who does not gather with Me scatters abroad.

³¹ "Therefore I say to you, every sin and blasphemy will be forgiven men, but the blasphemy against the Spirit will not be forgiven men. ³² Anyone who speaks a word against the Son of Man, it will be forgiven him; but whoever speaks against the Holy Spirit, it will not be forgiven him, either in this age or in the age to come."

7. How did the Pharisees try to explain Jesus' ability to drive out demons (see verse 24)?

_____

_____

_____

_____

8. How did Jesus respond to the Pharisees' accusations? What did He mean when He said, "Every kingdom divided against itself is brought to desolation" (verse 25)?

_____

_____

_____

_____

REVIEWING THE STORY

Jesus' ministry challenged everyone who encountered it. His disciples were challenged to risk their comfort and security to carry His message to distant places. John the Baptist was challenged to confront his doubts and misunderstandings about Jesus being the Messiah. The Pharisees were challenged to face their hypocrisy when they falsely accused Jesus of violating Sabbath laws and possessing demonic power. Yet Jesus answered each challenge that was brought against His ministry. He warned and equipped His disciples to carry His message to the world. He encouraged John the Baptist and confirmed that He was the Messiah. He rebutted and rejected the Pharisees' accusations. For every challenge . . . Jesus had a response.

9. What challenge did Jesus give to those who believed following Him would prevent conflict and trouble in their lives (see Matthew 10:16–20)?

_____

_____

_____

10. How did Jesus reassure John the Baptist in his moment of doubt (see Matthew 11:4–6)?

11. What did the Pharisees do when they realized that they were no match for Jesus in religious debates (see Matthew 12:14)?

12. What does blasphemy against the Holy Spirit look like? Why do you think Jesus said it was the only sin that would not be forgiven (see Matthew 12:31–33)?

APPLYING THE MESSAGE

13. How has Jesus sent you out into the world? What does it look like for you to proclaim His message?

14. What are some doubts that you've had about Jesus' desire or ability to work in your life? How is Jesus working in your life today?

Reflecting on the Meaning

Before Jesus sends us out, He equips us. He gives us everything we need to carry out the work He has prepared for us. However, it may not always *seem* like we're fully equipped. As Jesus warned His disciples, as His followers we will face situations and circumstances that take us out of our comfort zones and make us rely on Him for strength, wisdom, and courage. Jesus will give us missions that are thrilling and daunting . . . but at times will feel overwhelming.

People will oppose us. Jesus' message has unpopular implications. It challenges others' understanding of their own goodness and self-sufficiency. It can seem narrow-minded and intolerant. When we are sent out by Jesus, people will question our motives, our character, and our intelligence. There will be seasons of our lives when telling people about Jesus is easy, and there will be seasons when it will be a struggle. We may get discouraged and doubtful. We may go through times when we forget and lose sight of our mission. When we face rejection, we may even start to wonder if following Jesus is really worth it.

That's why Jesus sent out His disciples in pairs. There's strength in numbers. God designed us to live and work as a community. We gather together for encouragement, companionship, and accountability. We're members of a family with a mission.

Journaling Your Response

What's the biggest challenge you face when doing Jesus' work in the world?

THE GREATEST STORIES EVER TOLD

Matthew 13:1–15:39

GETTING STARTED

Is there a book or movie you have trouble understanding? What made the story so confusing?

_____

_____

_____

_____

_____

_____

_____

_____

_____

_____

_____

_____

_____

_____

_____

_____

_____

_____

SETTING THE STAGE

Stories are powerful. We embrace them, reflect on them, and let them move us to action. Jesus understood the power of stories. He often used the familiar images of His day, such as a fig tree or a farmer sowing seeds, to illustrate profound spiritual truths. As a storyteller, Jesus had no equal. His parables painted a picture of what it looked like to live out God's design for humanity.

However, Jesus didn't start His ministry teaching in parables. His use of parables marked a sudden shift in His teaching style—and one that initially confused His followers. At one point, His disciples even asked, "Why do you speak to the people in parables?" (Matthew 13:10). Jesus' explanation recalled His confrontation with the Pharisees over a demon-possessed man (see 12:22–32). Everyone had seen the miraculous healing, yet they all interpreted it differently. Some in the crowd took the event as proof that Jesus was the Messiah.

Yet even though the Pharisees had devoted their lives to the study of the Law and the writings of the prophets, they were unwilling and unable to admit that Jesus was sent by God. Their hearts were hardened, and they instantly rejected Jesus' words and actions. There was no way His message could take root in their hearts, so Jesus stopped trying. Instead, He embraced stories and parables that would force His listeners to carefully think about and consider His message. Only those who were truly open to His words would understand His teachings.

EXPLORING THE TEXT

The Parable of the Sower (Matthew 13:3–23)

³ Then He spoke many things to them in parables, saying: "Behold, a sower went out to sow. ⁴ And as he sowed, some seed fell by the wayside; and the birds came and devoured them. ⁵ Some fell on stony places, where they did not have much earth; and they immediately

sprang up because they had no depth of earth. [6] But when the sun was up they were scorched, and because they had no root they withered away. [7] And some fell among thorns, and the thorns sprang up and choked them. [8] But others fell on good ground and yielded a crop: some a hundredfold, some sixty, some thirty. [9] He who has ears to hear, let him hear!"

[10] And the disciples came and said to Him, "Why do You speak to them in parables?"

[11] He answered and said to them, "Because it has been given to you to know the mysteries of the kingdom of heaven, but to them it has not been given. [12] For whoever has, to him more will be given, and he will have abundance; but whoever does not have, even what he has will be taken away from him. [13] Therefore I speak to them in parables, because seeing they do not see, and hearing they do not hear, nor do they understand. [14] And in them the prophecy of Isaiah is fulfilled, which says:

'Hearing you will hear and shall not understand,
And seeing you will see and not perceive;
[15] For the hearts of this people have grown dull.
Their ears are hard of hearing,
And their eyes they have closed,
Lest they should see with their eyes and hear with their ears,
Lest they should understand with their hearts and turn,
So that I should heal them.'

[16] But blessed are your eyes for they see, and your ears for they hear; [17] for assuredly, I say to you that many prophets and righteous men desired to see what you see, and did not see it, and to hear what you hear, and did not hear it.

[18] "Therefore hear the parable of the sower: [19] When anyone hears the word of the kingdom, and does not understand it, then the wicked one comes and snatches away what was sown in his heart. This is he

who received seed by the wayside. [20] But he who received the seed on stony places, this is he who hears the word and immediately receives it with joy; [21] yet he has no root in himself, but endures only for a while. For when tribulation or persecution arises because of the word, immediately he stumbles. [22] Now he who received seed among the thorns is he who hears the word, and the cares of this world and the deceitfulness of riches choke the word, and he becomes unfruitful. [23] But he who received seed on the good ground is he who hears the word and understands it, who indeed bears fruit and produces: some a hundredfold, some sixty, some thirty."

---

1. In the parable of the sower, where did the seeds fall? Where were the seeds able to take root and grow in a healthy way (see verses 3–9)?

_____

_____

_____

_____

2. How did Jesus respond to the disciples' question about why He spoke to the people in parables? Why did Jesus call the disciples "blessed" (verse 16)?

_____

_____

_____

_____

Parables of the Kingdom of Heaven (Matthew 13:44–52)

[44] "Again, the kingdom of heaven is like treasure hidden in a field, which a man found and hid; and for joy over it he goes and sells all that he has and buys that field.

⁴⁵ "Again, the kingdom of heaven is like a merchant seeking beautiful pearls, ⁴⁶ who, when he had found one pearl of great price, went and sold all that he had and bought it.

⁴⁷ "Again, the kingdom of heaven is like a dragnet that was cast into the sea and gathered some of every kind, ⁴⁸ which, when it was full, they drew to shore; and they sat down and gathered the good into vessels, but threw the bad away. ⁴⁹ So it will be at the end of the age. The angels will come forth, separate the wicked from among the just, ⁵⁰ and cast them into the furnace of fire. There will be wailing and gnashing of teeth."

⁵¹ Jesus said to them, "Have you understood all these things?"
They said to Him, "Yes, Lord."

⁵² Then He said to them, "Therefore every scribe instructed concerning the kingdom of heaven is like a householder who brings out of his treasure things new and old."

3. What did Jesus want His audience to understand about God's kingdom through the three parables He told (see verses 44–50)?

_____
_____
_____
_____

4. What did Jesus imply was the disciples' responsibility in communicating these truths about the kingdom of heaven to others (see verse 52)?

_____
_____
_____
_____
_____

Jesus Walks on the Water (Matthew 14:22–33)

22 Immediately Jesus made His disciples get into the boat and go before Him to the other side, while He sent the multitudes away. 23 And when He had sent the multitudes away, He went up on the mountain by Himself to pray. Now when evening came, He was alone there. 24 But the boat was now in the middle of the sea, tossed by the waves, for the wind was contrary.

25 Now in the fourth watch of the night Jesus went to them, walking on the sea. 26 And when the disciples saw Him walking on the sea, they were troubled, saying, "It is a ghost!" And they cried out for fear.

27 But immediately Jesus spoke to them, saying, "Be of good cheer! It is I; do not be afraid."

28 And Peter answered Him and said, "Lord, if it is You, command me to come to You on the water."

29 So He said, "Come." And when Peter had come down out of the boat, he walked on the water to go to Jesus. 30 But when he saw that the wind was boisterous, he was afraid; and beginning to sink he cried out, saying, "Lord, save me!"

31 And immediately Jesus stretched out His hand and caught him, and said to him, "O you of little faith, why did you doubt?" 32 And when they got into the boat, the wind ceased.

33 Then those who were in the boat came and worshiped Him, saying, "Truly You are the Son of God."

---

5. What are some reasons why Jesus might have "made His disciples get into the boat" (verse 22) and sail without Him to the other side of the lake?

_____

_____

_____

6. How did Peter demonstrate his faith in Jesus? What caused him to sink (see verses 28–31)?

_____

_____

_____

_____

_____

Defilement Comes from Within (Matthew 15:1–20)

¹ Then the scribes and Pharisees who were from Jerusalem came to Jesus, saying, ² "Why do Your disciples transgress the tradition of the elders? For they do not wash their hands when they eat bread."

³ He answered and said to them, "Why do you also transgress the commandment of God because of your tradition? ⁴ For God commanded, saying, 'Honor your father and your mother'; and, 'He who curses father or mother, let him be put to death.' ⁵ But you say, 'Whoever says to his father or mother, "Whatever profit you might have received from me is a gift to God"— ⁶ then he need not honor his father or mother.' Thus you have made the commandment of God of no effect by your tradition. ⁷ Hypocrites! Well did Isaiah prophesy about you, saying:

⁸ 'These people draw near to Me with their mouth,
And honor Me with their lips,
But their heart is far from Me.
⁹ And in vain they worship Me,
Teaching as doctrines the commandments of men.' "

¹⁰ When He had called the multitude to Himself, He said to them, "Hear and understand: ¹¹ Not what goes into the mouth defiles a man; but what comes out of the mouth, this defiles a man."

¹² Then His disciples came and said to Him, "Do You know that the Pharisees were offended when they heard this saying?"

¹³ But He answered and said, "Every plant which My heavenly Father has not planted will be uprooted. ¹⁴ Let them alone. They are blind leaders of the blind. And if the blind leads the blind, both will fall into a ditch."

¹⁵ Then Peter answered and said to Him, "Explain this parable to us."

¹⁶ So Jesus said, "Are you also still without understanding? ¹⁷ Do you not yet understand that whatever enters the mouth goes into the stomach and is eliminated? ¹⁸ But those things which proceed out of the mouth come from the heart, and they defile a man. ¹⁹ For out of the heart proceed evil thoughts, murders, adulteries, fornications, thefts, false witness, blasphemies. ²⁰ These are the things which defile a man, but to eat with unwashed hands does not defile a man."

---

7. Why was Jesus so upset with the scribes and Pharisees (see verses 3–9)?

_____

_____

_____

_____

8. The Pharisees believed eating without ceremonially cleansing one's hands made a person unclean. According to Jesus, what *really* made a person unclean (see verses 11, 16–20)?

_____

_____

_____

_____

_____

REVIEWING THE STORY

Matthew 13–15 records a variety of reactions to Jesus' ministry and message. Jesus' preaching and teaching created confusion, disapproval, skepticism, astonishment, and even sheer terror! His parables baffled His followers, and His refusal to follow ceremonial law angered the Pharisees. When Jesus returned to His hometown of Nazareth, the people there refused to believe He was anything more than a carpenter's son. However, the astonished crowds who witnessed His miracles knew better. When they saw His power, they knew He was sent by God.

9. In Jesus' explanation of the parable of the sower, He gives three reasons why the word of the kingdom wouldn't bear fruit in a person's life. What are those reasons (see Matthew 13:19–22)?

_____

_____

_____

_____

_____

_____

10. Jesus' parables of the kingdom of heaven reveal that those who accept His message find a treasure beyond all price (see Matthew 13:44–46). How did the disciples reveal through their lives that they "understood all these things" (verse 51)?

_____

_____

_____

_____

_____

_____

11. How did Jesus demonstrate to the disciples that He would be with them during even the greatest crises in their lives (see Matthew 14:25–27)?

_____

_____

_____

_____

_____

_____

12. What charges did Jesus level against the Pharisees? Why did He feel they were being hypocritical in their approach to following God's laws (see Matthew 15:3–6)?

_____

_____

_____

_____

_____

_____

APPLYING THE MESSAGE

13. How would you describe the condition of the "soil" in your heart right now?

_____

_____

_____

_____

_____

_____

14. The disciples consistently forgot the many miracles that Jesus had done. Just before they set sail across the Sea of Galilee, Jesus had fed thousands of people . . . but they couldn't believe it when they saw Him walking on the water! What does it look like for you to forget what Jesus has done in the past? What can you do to better remember?

_____

_____

_____

_____

_____

_____

REFLECTING ON THE MEANING

Peter didn't fail on the Sea of Gennesaret. In fact, he was the only disciple who *didn't* fail because he was the only one willing to get out of the boat. The other disciples only saw darkness and danger in the storm. However, Peter saw Jesus—and that was all he needed. Peter's faith gives us an example to follow as we take bold risks for Jesus.

First, Peter *made sure he understood what Jesus wanted*. "Lord," he requested, "if it is You, command me to come to You on the water" (Matthew 14:28). Peter only proceeded after Jesus said, "Come." When Jesus gave the command, Peter then *didn't hesitate to step out of the boat*. He didn't wait for someone else to join him or debate the pros and cons. As soon as Jesus called him, Peter stepped out of the boat and "walked on the water to go to Jesus" (verse 30).

As Peter did (for a moment, at least), he *kept his focus on Christ*. The wind howled and the waves crashed, but they didn't stop his progress—until he paid attention to them. As soon as Peter took his focus off Jesus, he became vulnerable to his circumstances—and he started to sink! It was at this point that Peter *asked Jesus for help*. When he did, Jesus immediately caught his disciple and helped him back to the boat.

Given the choice between the comfort of the boat and the risk of the water, Peter chose the water—and was rewarded with a life-changing experience. For the rest of their lives, the other eleven disciples would speak with awe about that night . . . but only one could reminisce about what it was actually like to walk on the water with Jesus.

JOURNALING YOUR RESPONSE

When was the last time you "stepped out of your boat" and did something spiritually challenging? What happened? How did it grow or change your faith?

"WHO DO YOU SAY I AM?"

Matthew 16:1–17:27

GETTING STARTED

Think about your last spiritual "mountaintop" experience and your last spiritual "valley" experience. What made the mountaintop experience so good and rewarding? What made the valley experience so difficult and challenging?

_____

_____

_____

_____

_____

_____

_____

_____

_____

_____

_____

_____

_____

_____

_____

_____

SETTING THE STAGE

Jesus had spent the last two and a half years preaching and teaching, and His mission was almost complete. He knew that His death on the cross was near. So He began to prepare His disciples for what they would see and experience during the final portion of His ministry.

As part of this preparation, at one point Jesus invited His three closest friends—Peter, James, and John—to climb to the top of a mountain with Him. In an instant, Jesus was transformed, and His three disciples saw Him as not just their human friend and teacher, but also as God's Son. While they looked on in astonishment, Moses and Elijah (two of the greatest and most revered individuals in Jewish history) appeared with Jesus and talked with Him about His impending death. At the top of the mountain, Jesus' three closest friends were given an unprecedented glimpse of His glory.

The experience continued to inspire and awe Peter years later. In his second epistle, he would write, "For we did not follow cunningly devised fables when we made known to you the power and coming of our Lord Jesus Christ, but were eyewitnesses of His majesty. For He received from God the Father honor and glory when such a voice came to Him from the Excellent Glory: 'This is My beloved Son, in whom I am well pleased.' And we heard this voice which came from heaven when we were with Him on the holy mountain" (2 Peter 1:16–18). Peter could testify about Jesus' majesty and glory because he had seen it with his own eyes.

EXPLORING THE TEXT

The Pharisees and Sadducees Seek a Sign (Matthew 16:1–12)

¹ Then the Pharisees and Sadducees came, and testing Him asked that He would show them a sign from heaven. ² He answered and said to them, "When it is evening you say, 'It will be fair weather, for the sky is red'; ³ and in the morning, 'It will be foul weather today,

for the sky is red and threatening.' Hypocrites! You know how to discern the face of the sky, but you cannot discern the signs of the times. ⁴ A wicked and adulterous generation seeks after a sign, and no sign shall be given to it except the sign of the prophet Jonah." And He left them and departed.

⁵ Now when His disciples had come to the other side, they had forgotten to take bread. ⁶ Then Jesus said to them, "Take heed and beware of the leaven of the Pharisees and the Sadducees."

⁷ And they reasoned among themselves, saying, "It is because we have taken no bread."

⁸ But Jesus, being aware of it, said to them, "O you of little faith, why do you reason among yourselves because you have brought no bread? ⁹ Do you not yet understand, or remember the five loaves of the five thousand and how many baskets you took up? ¹⁰ Nor the seven loaves of the four thousand and how many large baskets you took up? ¹¹ How is it you do not understand that I did not speak to you concerning bread?—but to beware of the leaven of the Pharisees and Sadducees." ¹² Then they understood that He did not tell them to beware of the leaven of bread, but of the doctrine of the Pharisees and Sadducees.

---

1. The "sign of Jonah" refers to the Old Testament prophet's visit to Nineveh. When the Ninevites heard Jonah's warnings, they realized his words came from the God who had saved him from death. Jonah himself was the sign, and the people heeded his warnings and repented (see Jonah 3:1–10). What message do you think Jesus was sending to the Pharisees and Sadducees when He referred to the sign of Jonah (see Matthew 16:4)?

_____

_____

_____

_____

_____

2. How did the disciples interpret Jesus' instruction to "beware of the leaven of the Pharisees and the Sadducees" (verse 6)? How did Jesus correct their understanding (see verses 7–11)?

_____

_____

_____

_____

_____

Peter Confesses Jesus As the Christ (Matthew 16:13–28)

13 When Jesus came into the region of Caesarea Philippi, He asked His disciples, saying, "Who do men say that I, the Son of Man, am?"

14 So they said, "Some say John the Baptist, some Elijah, and others Jeremiah or one of the prophets."

15 He said to them, "But who do you say that I am?"

16 Simon Peter answered and said, "You are the Christ, the Son of the living God."

17 Jesus answered and said to him, "Blessed are you, Simon Bar-Jonah, for flesh and blood has not revealed this to you, but My Father who is in heaven. 18 And I also say to you that you are Peter, and on this rock I will build My church, and the gates of Hades shall not prevail against it. 19 And I will give you the keys of the kingdom of heaven, and whatever you bind on earth will be bound in heaven, and whatever you loose on earth will be loosed in heaven."

20 Then He commanded His disciples that they should tell no one that He was Jesus the Christ.

21 From that time Jesus began to show to His disciples that He must go to Jerusalem, and suffer many things from the elders and chief priests and scribes, and be killed, and be raised the third day.

22 Then Peter took Him aside and began to rebuke Him, saying, "Far be it from You, Lord; this shall not happen to You!"

²³ But He turned and said to Peter, "Get behind Me, Satan! You are an offense to Me, for you are not mindful of the things of God, but the things of men."

²⁴ Then Jesus said to His disciples, "If anyone desires to come after Me, let him deny himself, and take up his cross, and follow Me. ²⁵ For whoever desires to save his life will lose it, but whoever loses his life for My sake will find it. ²⁶ For what profit is it to a man if he gains the whole world, and loses his own soul? Or what will a man give in exchange for his soul? ²⁷ For the Son of Man will come in the glory of His Father with His angels, and then He will reward each according to his works. ²⁸ Assuredly, I say to you, there are some standing here who shall not taste death till they see the Son of Man coming in His kingdom."

---

3. How did the crowds who followed Jesus view Him (see verse 14)?

_____

_____

_____

_____

_____

4. Peter was the first of the apostles to acknowledge that Jesus was the Messiah . . . and he was probably the first person to realize that whatever happened to Jesus likely would happen to His disciples as well. How does that change the way you view Peter's words in verse 22? How does that change the way you view Jesus' rebuke in verses 23–28?

_____

_____

_____

_____

Jesus Transfigured on the Mount (Matthew 17:1–9)

[1] Now after six days Jesus took Peter, James, and John his brother, led them up on a high mountain by themselves; [2] and He was transfigured before them. His face shone like the sun, and His clothes became as white as the light. [3] And behold, Moses and Elijah appeared to them, talking with Him. [4] Then Peter answered and said to Jesus, "Lord, it is good for us to be here; if You wish, let us make here three tabernacles: one for You, one for Moses, and one for Elijah."

[5] While he was still speaking, behold, a bright cloud overshadowed them; and suddenly a voice came out of the cloud, saying, "This is My beloved Son, in whom I am well pleased. Hear Him!" [6] And when the disciples heard it, they fell on their faces and were greatly afraid. [7] But Jesus came and touched them and said, "Arise, and do not be afraid." [8] When they had lifted up their eyes, they saw no one but Jesus only.

[9] Now as they came down from the mountain, Jesus commanded them, saying, "Tell the vision to no one until the Son of Man is risen from the dead."

5. Review 2 Peter 1:16–18. Peter wrote those words almost *forty years* after these events took place on the mountain. How did Peter's experience on top of the mountain impact the rest of his life—and the lives of James and John?

_____

_____

_____

_____

_____

_____

6. After Jesus' baptism, a voice from heaven declared, "This is My beloved Son, in whom I am well pleased" (Matthew 3:17). Why do you think God chose to repeat this same affirmation to Jesus at this particular time in His life?

_____

_____

_____

_____

_____

_____

_____

_____

_____

A Boy Is Healed (Matthew 17:14–23)

¹⁴ And when they had come to the multitude, a man came to Him, kneeling down to Him and saying, ¹⁵ "Lord, have mercy on my son, for he is an epileptic and suffers severely; for he often falls into the fire and often into the water. ¹⁶ So I brought him to Your disciples, but they could not cure him."

¹⁷ Then Jesus answered and said, "O faithless and perverse generation, how long shall I be with you? How long shall I bear with you? Bring him here to Me." ¹⁸ And Jesus rebuked the demon, and it came out of him; and the child was cured from that very hour.

¹⁹ Then the disciples came to Jesus privately and said, "Why could we not cast it out?"

²⁰ So Jesus said to them, "Because of your unbelief; for assuredly, I say to you, if you have faith as a mustard seed, you will say to this mountain, 'Move from here to there,' and it will move; and nothing will be impossible for you. ²¹ However, this kind does not go out except by prayer and fasting."

²² Now while they were staying in Galilee, Jesus said to them, "The Son of Man is about to be betrayed into the hands of men, ²³ and they will kill Him, and the third day He will be raised up." And they were exceedingly sorrowful.

---

7. Why do you think Jesus reacted so strongly when He learned the disciples were unable to cast the demon out of the boy (see verses 17–18)?

_____

_____

_____

_____

_____

_____

_____

_____

_____

8. What does Jesus say about the power of faith in this passage (see verse 20)?

_____

_____

_____

_____

_____

_____

_____

_____

_____

REVIEWING THE STORY

The Pharisees and Sadducees saw Jesus perform several miracles, but they demanded more. Jesus knew their hearts, so He refused to "perform" for them. Peter had seen Christ enact the same astounding miracles, but he was able to recognize what they meant: Jesus was the promised Messiah, the Son of God. However, even though Peter understood who Jesus was, he didn't understand what Jesus came to do—which was why he wouldn't listen to his Lord talk about His death. Later, during the Transfiguration, Peter, James, and John would get a glimpse of Jesus' power and glory as the Son of God. But immediately afterward they would witness the limits of their own power when they were unable to heal the demon-possessed boy.

9. What "test" did the Pharisees and Sadducees give to Jesus (see Matthew 16:1)?

_____

_____

_____

_____

_____

_____

10. Why do you think Peter rebuked Jesus for talking about His death (see Matthew 16:22)?

_____

_____

_____

_____

_____

_____

_____

11. What did Peter, James, and John see during the Transfiguration (see Matthew 17:1–6)?

_____

_____

_____

_____

_____

_____

12. Why were the disciples unable to cast the demon out of the boy (see Matthew 17:20–21)?

_____

_____

_____

_____

_____

_____

_____

APPLYING THE MESSAGE

13. Who do you say Jesus is? What does that mean to you?

_____

_____

_____

_____

_____

_____

14. Do Jesus' words in Matthew 17:20–21 encourage you or discourage you? Why?

_____

_____

_____

_____

_____

_____

_____

REFLECTING ON THE MEANING

In Matthew 16–17, Peter's faith follows a pattern we have all experienced. He has an extraordinary spiritual triumph (a spiritual "high point") followed by an equally extraordinary lapse of judgment (a spiritual "low point"). In one moment, he shows stunning insight by identifying Jesus as the Messiah, the Son of the living God. In response to his faith, Jesus calls him "blessed." However, in the very next paragraph, Jesus tells His disciples that He is going to suffer and die when He gets to Jerusalem. And what does Peter do? He pulls Jesus aside and tells Him that nothing like that will ever happen to Him.

Jesus' response is swift and sharp: "Get behind Me, Satan! You are an offense to Me, for you are not mindful of the things of God, but the things of men" (Matthew 16:23). For Peter, to go from being called "blessed" to being called "Satan" in the same conversation would represent a pretty abrupt change from spiritual high to spiritual low.

Many of us have the same experience. As we follow Jesus, we grow, become more mature, and understand more about who Jesus is and how He changes our lives . . . only to get tripped up by something else. We alternate between wisdom and foolishness, holiness and sin, maturity and immaturity. The reality is that this is normal. We live in a world that is broken. We have sin that lives within us, and there are seasons of our lives where we will fight and triumph and where we will fight and fail.

On top of our own sin, we have a spiritual enemy. When we experience a spiritual high, there is nothing Satan wants to do more than bring us down, crush us, and make us feel like a failure. Between the broken world we live in, our sinful inclinations, and our spiritual enemy, it's easy for us to go from spiritual high to spiritual low.

The good news is that God's love for us isn't determined by whether we feel like we are in the middle of a spiritual high or spiritual low. Peter's wisdom or foolishness didn't change the fact that he was still one of Jesus' disciples and friends. When we understand that peaks and valleys are a natural part of following Jesus, and that they don't change our relationship with God, we are able to walk and grow through them!

JOURNALING YOUR RESPONSE

How does your relationship with God change during a spiritually high season? How does it change during a season of spiritual lows? How have you grown in both seasons?

REDEFINING GREATNESS

Matthew 18:1–20:34

GETTING STARTED

Who is the greatest person you know? What makes that person great in your eyes?

SETTING THE STAGE

Jesus' talk about His coming kingdom stirred political ambitions among His disciples. On more than one occasion, they argued about which of them would rule next to Jesus on His throne. The debate centered on which of them was the *greatest*. Since they had been with Jesus from the start of His ministry, they anticipated receiving exalted positions in Jesus' kingdom. After all, they reasoned, it's not *what* you know but *who* you know.

However, in this case, it was what the disciples *didn't* know that thwarted their ambitions. For one thing, they did not understand the nature of Jesus' kingdom. They saw Jesus as a political Messiah—an avenging warrior who would throw off Israel's shackles of Roman occupation and re-establish their national sovereignty. The disciples envisioned an earthly kingdom filled with opportunities for personal glory and political gain. They thought Jesus' kingdom would be established sooner rather than later, so they jockeyed for position.

What the disciples didn't understand was that Jesus' kingdom wasn't an earthly, political kingdom but a spiritual one—an eternal kingdom— that would be far greater than anything they could imagine. Only God the Father knew when it would be established. But that wasn't all the disciples didn't understand. The disciples also didn't know what *qualified* someone for a position of honor in Jesus' kingdom. They didn't realize just how different their definition of *greatness* was from Jesus' definition. They didn't understand that to reach the exalted positions they craved, they had to empty themselves of ambition and embrace servanthood.

EXPLORING THE TEXT

Who Is the Greatest? (Matthew 18:1–14)

---

¹ At that time the disciples came to Jesus, saying, "Who then is greatest in the kingdom of heaven?"

[2] Then Jesus called a little child to Him, set him in the midst of them, [3] and said, "Assuredly, I say to you, unless you are converted and become as little children, you will by no means enter the kingdom of heaven. [4] Therefore whoever humbles himself as this little child is the greatest in the kingdom of heaven. [5] Whoever receives one little child like this in My name receives Me.

[6] "But whoever causes one of these little ones who believe in Me to sin, it would be better for him if a millstone were hung around his neck, and he were drowned in the depth of the sea. [7] Woe to the world because of offenses! For offenses must come, but woe to that man by whom the offense comes!

[8] "If your hand or foot causes you to sin, cut it off and cast it from you. It is better for you to enter into life lame or maimed, rather than having two hands or two feet, to be cast into the everlasting fire. [9] And if your eye causes you to sin, pluck it out and cast it from you. It is better for you to enter into life with one eye, rather than having two eyes, to be cast into hell fire.

[10] "Take heed that you do not despise one of these little ones, for I say to you that in heaven their angels always see the face of My Father who is in heaven. [11] For the Son of Man has come to save that which was lost.

[12] "What do you think? If a man has a hundred sheep, and one of them goes astray, does he not leave the ninety-nine and go to the mountains to seek the one that is straying? [13] And if he should find it, assuredly, I say to you, he rejoices more over that sheep than over the ninety-nine that did not go astray. [14] Even so it is not the will of your Father who is in heaven that one of these little ones should perish."

---

1. Why do you think Jesus talked about children when His disciples asked Him who was greatest in the kingdom of heaven (see verses 1–7)?

2. What was the point of Jesus' parable about the lost sheep (see verses 12–14)? What does this tell you about the way God values every person?

_____

_____

_____

_____

_____

Marriage and Divorce (Matthew 19:1–12)

¹ Now it came to pass, when Jesus had finished these sayings, that He departed from Galilee and came to the region of Judea beyond the Jordan. ² And great multitudes followed Him, and He healed them there.

³ The Pharisees also came to Him, testing Him, and saying to Him, "Is it lawful for a man to divorce his wife for just any reason?"

⁴ And He answered and said to them, "Have you not read that He who made them at the beginning 'made them male and female,' ⁵ and said, 'For this reason a man shall leave his father and mother and be joined to his wife, and the two shall become one flesh'? ⁶ So then, they are no longer two but one flesh. Therefore what God has joined together, let not man separate."

⁷ They said to Him, "Why then did Moses command to give a certificate of divorce, and to put her away?"

⁸ He said to them, "Moses, because of the hardness of your hearts, permitted you to divorce your wives, but from the beginning it was not so. ⁹ And I say to you, whoever divorces his wife, except for sexual immorality, and marries another, commits adultery; and whoever marries her who is divorced commits adultery."

¹⁰ His disciples said to Him, "If such is the case of the man with his wife, it is better not to marry."

¹¹ But He said to them, "All cannot accept this saying, but only those to whom it has been given: ¹² For there are eunuchs who were

born thus from their mother's womb, and there are eunuchs who were made eunuchs by men, and there are eunuchs who have made themselves eunuchs for the kingdom of heaven's sake. He who is able to accept it, let him accept it."

---

3. What reason did Jesus give for why divorce was allowed in the Old Testament? What did Jesus instruct about the practice of divorce (see verses 7–8)?

_____

_____

_____

_____

_____

_____

_____

_____

4. Read 1 Corinthians 7:5–9. In what ways are Paul's instructions to believers similar to Jesus' words to His disciples in this passage (see Matthew 19:11–12)?

_____

_____

_____

_____

_____

_____

_____

_____

Jesus Counsels the Rich Young Ruler (Matthew 19:16–30)

¹⁶ Now behold, one came and said to Him, "Good Teacher, what good thing shall I do that I may have eternal life?"

¹⁷ So He said to him, "Why do you call Me good? No one is good but One, that is, God. But if you want to enter into life, keep the commandments."

¹⁸ He said to Him, "Which ones?"

Jesus said, "'You shall not murder,' 'You shall not commit adultery,' 'You shall not steal,' 'You shall not bear false witness,' ¹⁹ 'Honor your father and your mother,' and, 'You shall love your neighbor as yourself.' "

²⁰ The young man said to Him, "All these things I have kept from my youth. What do I still lack?"

²¹ Jesus said to him, "If you want to be perfect, go, sell what you have and give to the poor, and you will have treasure in heaven; and come, follow Me."

²² But when the young man heard that saying, he went away sorrowful, for he had great possessions.

²³ Then Jesus said to His disciples, "Assuredly, I say to you that it is hard for a rich man to enter the kingdom of heaven. ²⁴ And again I say to you, it is easier for a camel to go through the eye of a needle than for a rich man to enter the kingdom of God."

²⁵ When His disciples heard it, they were greatly astonished, saying, "Who then can be saved?"

²⁶ But Jesus looked at them and said to them, "With men this is impossible, but with God all things are possible."

²⁷ Then Peter answered and said to Him, "See, we have left all and followed You. Therefore what shall we have?"

²⁸ So Jesus said to them, "Assuredly I say to you, that in the regeneration, when the Son of Man sits on the throne of His glory, you who have followed Me will also sit on twelve thrones, judging the twelve tribes of Israel. ²⁹ And everyone who has left houses or

brothers or sisters or father or mother or wife or children or lands, for My name's sake, shall receive a hundredfold, and inherit eternal life. [30] But many who are first will be last, and the last first."

---

5. In Jesus' reply to the rich young man, He named six of the ten commandments. One of the commandments that Jesus *didn't* mention was the first one: "You shall have no other gods before Me" (Exodus 20:3). What connection do you see between that commandment and Jesus' instruction for the young man to sell everything he possessed (see Matthew 19:21)?

_____

_____

_____

_____

6. Matthew writes that the young man "went away sorrowful" (verse 22) . . . but he wasn't quite sorrowful *enough* to do what Jesus had told him to do if he really wanted eternal life. How do you explain the young man's reaction?

_____

_____

_____

_____

A Mother's Request (Matthew 20:17–28)

[17] Now Jesus, going up to Jerusalem, took the twelve disciples aside on the road and said to them, [18] "Behold, we are going up to Jerusalem, and the Son of Man will be betrayed to the chief priests and to the scribes; and they will condemn Him to death, [19] and deliver Him to the Gentiles to mock and to scourge and to crucify. And the third day He will rise again."

²⁰ Then the mother of Zebedee's sons came to Him with her sons, kneeling down and asking something from Him.

²¹ And He said to her, "What do you wish?"

She said to Him, "Grant that these two sons of mine may sit, one on Your right hand and the other on the left, in Your kingdom."

²² But Jesus answered and said, "You do not know what you ask. Are you able to drink the cup that I am about to drink, and be baptized with the baptism that I am baptized with?"

They said to Him, "We are able."

²³ So He said to them, "You will indeed drink My cup, and be baptized with the baptism that I am baptized with; but to sit on My right hand and on My left is not Mine to give, but it is for those for whom it is prepared by My Father."

²⁴ And when the ten heard it, they were greatly displeased with the two brothers. ²⁵ But Jesus called them to Himself and said, "You know that the rulers of the Gentiles lord it over them, and those who are great exercise authority over them. ²⁶ Yet it shall not be so among you; but whoever desires to become great among you, let him be your servant. ²⁷ And whoever desires to be first among you, let him be your slave— ²⁸ just as the Son of Man did not come to be served, but to serve, and to give His life a ransom for many."

---

7. Why do you think James' and John's mother made the request she did (see verses 20–21)?

_____

_____

_____

_____

_____

_____

_____

8. How did the other disciples react to her request (see verse 24)? What impact do you think this had on their relationship with James and John?

REVIEWING THE STORY

It's easy for us to fall into the trap of thinking greatness comes from power, wealth, or our own position. After all, that is what the rest of the world thinks. However, the world's rules about greatness, power, and justice don't apply to Jesus' kingdom. In His kingdom, greatness comes from humility, power is achieved through a serving spirit, and justice is left up to God—our part is simply to offer mercy and forgiveness to those who have offended us. As followers of Jesus, we forgive others because *we* have received God's forgiveness. This forgiveness changes every relationship we have—with our spouse, in our family, with our friends, and at our jobs. In Jesus' kingdom, our relationships work the way God originally designed them to work!

9. How did Jesus define who is greatest in the kingdom of heaven (see Matthew 18:1–7)?

10. Based on Jesus' response to the Pharisees, how would you summarize His teachings on marriage and divorce (see Matthew 19:1–12)?

11. How does Jesus reward those who leave everything to follow Him (see Matthew 19:27–30)?

_____

_____

_____

_____

_____

_____

12. Who grants positions of authority and importance in Jesus' kingdom (see Matthew 20:23)? What did Jesus say was the "secret" to being great in God's kingdom (see verses 26–28)?

_____

_____

_____

_____

_____

_____

APPLYING THE MESSAGE

13. What does it look like for leaders to serve the people they lead instead of lording authority over them? How does this idea impact the way you lead?

_____

_____

_____

_____

_____

_____

14. The rich young ruler was unwilling to give up the security of his earthly possessions to wholeheartedly follow Christ. What gives you security in this world? How have you been able to put your trust completely in Jesus rather than the things of this world?

_____

_____

_____

_____

_____

_____

REFLECTING ON THE MEANING

The model of leadership and greatness that Jesus gave His followers is entirely opposite of the way the world operates. The traditional model of success is a triangle. The higher we rise, the fewer people there are above us. When we get to the top (the most desired position), we are alone. Everyone below us answers to us and serves us. We think success is based on how high we can climb and how many people we control. Up is good and down is bad.

However, in Jesus' model, service determines our success. The more people we serve, the greater—and more successful—we are. Jesus thus flips the triangle model upside down. To serve someone, we have to consider that person as better than us, greater than us, and worthy of our service. Pride, ego, competitiveness, greed, and the desire for power—the things that fuel the traditional model—have no place in Jesus' triangle. Humility, compassion, and love are the alternative fuels of His kingdom. Those are the qualities that get us to the bottom of the upside-down triangle. And as Jesus showed us through His life, death, and resurrection, the _bottom_ is where we find true greatness. If we want to be great, our focus has to be serving others. Greatness is found when we sacrifice our time, energy, and resources for others.

The apostle Paul summed up Jesus' understanding of leadership and greatness at the beginning of his letter to the church at Philippi, where he wrote, "Let this mind be in you which was also in Christ Jesus, who, being in the form of God, did not consider it robbery to be equal with God, but made Himself of no reputation, taking the form of a bondservant, and coming in the likeness of men (Philippians 2:5–7). If we want to know what it means to be great, all we have to do is look to the example of Jesus.

JOURNALING YOUR RESPONSE

What part of Jesus' instructions for leadership do you find easiest to follow? Which parts are the most difficult? Why?

THE ARRIVAL OF THE KING

Matthew 21:1–22:46

GETTING STARTED

How would you respond to someone who said that Jesus was not actually God? What evidence from the Bible would you use to make your point that He was fully divine?

_____

_____

_____

_____

_____

_____

_____

_____

_____

_____

SETTING THE STAGE

The people who crowded into Jerusalem for the Passover celebration understood they were part of something momentous. They were celebrating the grand story of God's faithfulness to Israel, just as their ancestors had done for generations before them. However, the final Passover of Jesus' life was even more significant. When Jesus entered the city, the crowds understood that He was more than just a teacher or holy man. Yet they didn't understand the eternal significance of the events that were unfolding in front of them.

Nor were they aware of the miracles that had preceded Jesus' arrival. The first miraculous event of the day involved Jesus' instructions to two of his disciples. He sent them to a nearby village, where He said they would find a donkey tied next to a colt. He told them to bring both animals to Him, saying, "And if anyone says anything to you, you shall say, 'The Lord has need of them,' and immediately he will send them" (Matthew 21:3). Jesus' words were bold, confident, and straightforward. They were the words of a leader, a man of authority—a King getting ready to usher in His kingdom. When the two disciples got to the village, they found a donkey tied with a colt, *exactly* as Jesus said they would.

The donkey and colt were clues. Anyone who understood Jewish prophecy would have recognized the implications of royalty in Jesus' choice of transportation. In Zechariah 9:9, the Old Testament prophet spoke of a future king who entered Jerusalem riding on a donkey. In Matthew 21, Jesus fully embraced His fulfillment of Zechariah's prophecy. That day, the multitudes in Jerusalem got a glimpse of the One whom the Jewish people had eagerly awaited for centuries—the Messiah, the Son of God.

EXPLORING THE TEXT

The Triumphal Entry (Matthew 21:1–11)

> [1] Now when they drew near Jerusalem, and came to Bethphage, at the Mount of Olives, then Jesus sent two disciples, [2] saying to them, "Go into the village opposite you, and immediately you will find a donkey tied, and a colt with her. Loose them and bring them to Me. [3] And if anyone says anything to you, you shall say, 'The Lord has need of them,' and immediately he will send them."

⁴ All this was done that it might be fulfilled which was spoken by the prophet, saying:

⁵ "Tell the daughter of Zion,
'Behold, your King is coming to you,
Lowly, and sitting on a donkey,
A colt, the foal of a donkey.' "

⁶ So the disciples went and did as Jesus commanded them. ⁷ They brought the donkey and the colt, laid their clothes on them, and set Him on them. ⁸ And a very great multitude spread their clothes on the road; others cut down branches from the trees and spread them on the road. ⁹ Then the multitudes who went before and those who followed cried out, saying:

"Hosanna to the Son of David!
'Blessed is He who comes in the name of the LORD!'
Hosanna in the highest!"

¹⁰ And when He had come into Jerusalem, all the city was moved, saying, "Who is this?"

¹¹ So the multitudes said, "This is Jesus, the prophet from Nazareth of Galilee."

---

1. What instructions did Jesus give to the disciples as they neared Jerusalem? For what reason does Matthew say that Jesus gave these specific instructions (see verses 1–5)?

_____

_____

_____

_____

2. How did the people react when they saw Jesus? How did they view Him (see verses 8–11)?

_____

_____

_____

_____

_____

_____

_____

_____

Jesus Overturns the Money Changers' Tables (Matthew 21:12–17)

¹² Then Jesus went into the temple of God and drove out all those who bought and sold in the temple, and overturned the tables of the money changers and the seats of those who sold doves. ¹³ And He said to them, "It is written, 'My house shall be called a house of prayer,' but you have made it a 'den of thieves.' "

¹⁴ Then the blind and the lame came to Him in the temple, and He healed them. ¹⁵ But when the chief priests and scribes saw the wonderful things that He did, and the children crying out in the temple and saying, "Hosanna to the Son of David!" they were indignant ¹⁶ and said to Him, "Do You hear what these are saying?"

And Jesus said to them, "Yes. Have you never read,

'Out of the mouth of babes and nursing infants
You have perfected praise'?"

¹⁷ Then He left them and went out of the city to Bethany, and He lodged there.

3. The money changers provided a service for pilgrims in converting the standard Greek and Roman currency into temple currency, from which the temple tax had to be paid. Likewise, the merchants sold doves for use in the temple sacrifices. Why do you think Jesus took issue with this type of trade taking place on the grounds of a holy place dedicated to God?

_____

_____

_____

_____

_____

_____

_____

4. What complaint did the chief priests and scribes in the temple have against Jesus? How did Jesus respond to their accusations (see verses 14–16)?

_____

_____

_____

_____

_____

_____

The Parable of the Wedding Feast (Matthew 22:1–14)

¹ And Jesus answered and spoke to them again by parables and said: ² "The kingdom of heaven is like a certain king who arranged a marriage for his son, ³ and sent out his servants to call those who were invited to the wedding; and they were not willing to come. ⁴ Again, he sent out other servants, saying, 'Tell those who are invited, "See, I have prepared my dinner; my oxen and fatted cattle are killed, and all things are ready. Come to the wedding." ' ⁵ But they made

light of it and went their ways, one to his own farm, another to his business. ⁶ And the rest seized his servants, treated them spitefully, and killed them. ⁷ But when the king heard about it, he was furious. And he sent out his armies, destroyed those murderers, and burned up their city. ⁸ Then he said to his servants, 'The wedding is ready, but those who were invited were not worthy. ⁹ Therefore go into the highways, and as many as you find, invite to the wedding.' ¹⁰ So those servants went out into the highways and gathered together all whom they found, both bad and good. And the wedding hall was filled with guests.

¹¹ "But when the king came in to see the guests, he saw a man there who did not have on a wedding garment. ¹² So he said to him, 'Friend, how did you come in here without a wedding garment?' And he was speechless. ¹³ Then the king said to the servants, 'Bind him hand and foot, take him away, and cast him into outer darkness; there will be weeping and gnashing of teeth.'

¹⁴ "For many are called, but few are chosen."

---

5. In Jesus' parable, the invited guests represent Israel, who rejected God's invitation of salvation through His Son. Who do the people on the highways—the ones who received the invitation after the initial guests rejected it—represent (see verses 8–10)?

_____

_____

_____

_____

_____

_____

_____

_____

6. Jesus notes that many are invited to the wedding feast, but some refuse to come. What happens to those who come but refuse to submit to God's laws (see verses 11–12)?

_____

_____

_____

_____

The Greatest Commandment (Matthew 22:23–40)

23 The same day the Sadducees, who say there is no resurrection, came to Him and asked Him, 24 saying: "Teacher, Moses said that if a man dies, having no children, his brother shall marry his wife and raise up offspring for his brother. 25 Now there were with us seven brothers. The first died after he had married, and having no offspring, left his wife to his brother. 26 Likewise the second also, and the third, even to the seventh. 27 Last of all the woman died also. 28 Therefore, in the resurrection, whose wife of the seven will she be? For they all had her."

29 Jesus answered and said to them, "You are mistaken, not knowing the Scriptures nor the power of God. 30 For in the resurrection they neither marry nor are given in marriage, but are like angels of God in heaven. 31 But concerning the resurrection of the dead, have you not read what was spoken to you by God, saying, 32 'I am the God of Abraham, the God of Isaac, and the God of Jacob'? God is not the God of the dead, but of the living." 33 And when the multitudes heard this, they were astonished at His teaching.

34 But when the Pharisees heard that He had silenced the Sadducees, they gathered together. 35 Then one of them, a lawyer, asked Him a question, testing Him, and saying, 36 "Teacher, which is the great commandment in the law?"

37 Jesus said to him, "'You shall love the LORD your God with all your heart, with all your soul, and with all your mind.' 38 This is the

first and great commandment. [39] And the second is like it: 'You shall love your neighbor as yourself.' [40] On these two commandments hang all the Law and the Prophets."

---

7. Why was it ironic that the Sadducees tried to trap Jesus using a question about the resurrection (see verses 23–28)?

_____

_____

_____

_____

_____

_____

_____

_____

8. How did the Pharisees try to stump Jesus? Why is it significant that a "lawyer" (one skilled in the Law of Moses) posed this question to Jesus (see verses 34–40)?

_____

_____

_____

_____

_____

REVIEWING THE STORY

Jesus faced opposition the moment He arrived in Jerusalem. The chief priests and elders questioned His authority. The Pharisees wanted to physically harm Him but feared how the crowds would react. The Sadducees tried to trip Him up with a nonsensical question about marriage in the resurrection. When their individual efforts failed, the Pharisees teamed up to question Jesus, and they asked Him which commandment in the Law was the greatest. However, no matter who opposed Jesus or how they approached Him, He saw through their attempts to oppose Him and overcame them.

9. Read Zechariah 9:9. What was the significance of Jesus entering Jerusalem riding a donkey? What was Jesus announcing at this time to the people (see Matthew 21:4–5)?

_____

_____

_____

_____

_____

_____

_____

_____

_____

10. According to Jesus, what was the true purpose of the temple (see Matthew 21:12–14)?

_____

_____

_____

_____

_____

_____

_____

_____

11. In the parable of the wedding feast, how did the different invited guests respond to the king's invitation (see Matthew 22:1–6)?

_____

_____

_____

_____

_____

_____

12. According to Jesus, what is the first and greatest commandment of the Law? What is the second greatest commandment (see Matthew 22:34–40)?

_____

_____

_____

_____

_____

_____

APPLYING THE MESSAGE

13. Which is easier for you to do: love God with all of your heart, soul, and mind, or love your neighbor as yourself? Why?

_____

_____

_____

_____

_____

_____

14. What does it look like for people to question Jesus' authority today?

_____

_____

_____

_____

_____

REFLECTING ON THE MEANING

When Jesus was asked to name the greatest commandment, He quoted Deuteronomy 6:5: "You shall love the LORD your God with all your heart, with all your soul, and with all your strength." But He changed the word _strength_ to _mind_: "You shall love the LORD your God with all your heart, with all your soul, and with all your mind" (Matthew 22:37).

What does that actually look like? It's easy for us to think that loving God with our mind means obtaining knowledge. However, loving God with our mind involves more than just absorbing information; it's also about letting that information change the way we live. We love God with our mind when we let His Word change us. When we fill our mind with God's Word, everything in our lives—our relationships, parenting choices, career paths, ethical decisions, morality—changes and starts to work the way God designed it to function.

When we love God with all our mind, we gain wisdom, which is the ability to apply the Word of God to the situations we face. Wisdom enables us to hear with God's ears and to see with God's eyes. With wisdom, we can understand God's nature, plan, and purpose.

That's what God wants from us. He doesn't want us to just know things about Him; He wants us to know Him and let that knowledge change us and make us look more like Him. The Pharisees who confronted Jesus knew about God, but that knowledge didn't change them. If we want to live the abundant life that Jesus has for us, we can't just let the Bible be a source of information. It has to be a catalyst for our transformation.

JOURNALING YOUR RESPONSE

Where have you turned God's Word into just a source of information? What would it look like for God's Word to cause real transformation in your life?

JESUS PREPARES HIS FOLLOWERS

Matthew 23:1–25:46

GETTING STARTED

If you knew that Jesus was going to return in one week, what would your to-do list for the next seven days look like?

_____

_____

_____

_____

_____

_____

_____

_____

_____

_____

_____

_____

_____

_____

_____

_____

_____

_____

SETTING THE STAGE

Jesus had pronounced a series of dire warnings to the Pharisees and the teachers of the Law for their hypocrisy. He spoke of coming judgment and warned that unless they changed their ways, they would not enter into the kingdom of God. This began a remarkable exchange between Jesus and His disciples about His kingdom and His second coming.

As the disciples were leaving the temple in Jerusalem, they called Jesus' attention to the beauty and enormity of the temple complex. Jesus' reply was provocative, to say the least. He told the disciples of a day in the future when the entire complex would be so utterly destroyed that not one stone would be left on top of another.

As expected, the disciples were shocked, intrigued, and wanted to know more. They asked Jesus three questions: When would this destruction of the temple occur? What would be the sign of His second coming? What would be the sign of the end of the age?

Jesus responded with a lengthy sermon in which He described God's coming judgment and His return in cosmic and apocalyptic terms. Just as the Old Testament prophets had described, the day of God's judgment would be a terrifying, earth-shaking day . . . but on the other side would be hope, peace, and a new way of living for God's people.

EXPLORING THE TEXT

Woe to the Scribes and Pharisees (Matthew 23:13–30)

---

13 "But woe to you, scribes and Pharisees, hypocrites! For you shut up the kingdom of heaven against men; for you neither go in yourselves, nor do you allow those who are entering to go in. 14 Woe to you, scribes and Pharisees, hypocrites! For you devour widows' houses, and for a pretense make long prayers. Therefore you will receive greater condemnation.

[15] "Woe to you, scribes and Pharisees, hypocrites! For you travel land and sea to win one proselyte, and when he is won, you make him twice as much a son of hell as yourselves.

[16] "Woe to you, blind guides, who say, 'Whoever swears by the temple, it is nothing; but whoever swears by the gold of the temple, he is obliged to perform it.' [17] Fools and blind! For which is greater, the gold or the temple that sanctifies the gold? [18] And, 'Whoever swears by the altar, it is nothing; but whoever swears by the gift that is on it, he is obliged to perform it.' [19] Fools and blind! For which is greater, the gift or the altar that sanctifies the gift? [20] Therefore he who swears by the altar, swears by it and by all things on it. [21] He who swears by the temple, swears by it and by Him who dwells in it. [22] And he who swears by heaven, swears by the throne of God and by Him who sits on it.

[23] "Woe to you, scribes and Pharisees, hypocrites! For you pay tithe of mint and anise and cummin, and have neglected the weightier matters of the law: justice and mercy and faith. These you ought to have done, without leaving the others undone. [24] Blind guides, who strain out a gnat and swallow a camel!

[25] "Woe to you, scribes and Pharisees, hypocrites! For you cleanse the outside of the cup and dish, but inside they are full of extortion and self-indulgence. [26] Blind Pharisee, first cleanse the inside of the cup and dish, that the outside of them may be clean also.

[27] "Woe to you, scribes and Pharisees, hypocrites! For you are like whitewashed tombs which indeed appear beautiful outwardly, but inside are full of dead men's bones and all uncleanness. [28] Even so you also outwardly appear righteous to men, but inside you are full of hypocrisy and lawlessness.

[29] "Woe to you, scribes and Pharisees, hypocrites! Because you build the tombs of the prophets and adorn the monuments of the righteous, [30] and say, 'If we had lived in the days of our fathers, we would not have been partakers with them in the blood of the prophets.' "

1. What are some of the main complaints that Jesus had against the scribes and the Pharisees? Which of these seven "woes" of Jesus stands out to you the most?

_____

_____

_____

_____

_____

2. Why do you think Jesus felt compelled to call out these actions of the scribes and the Pharisees? How were they blocking people from finding the kingdom of heaven?

_____

_____

_____

_____

_____

Jesus Predicts the Temple's Destruction (Matthew 24:1–28)

¹ Then Jesus went out and departed from the temple, and His disciples came up to show Him the buildings of the temple. ² And Jesus said to them, "Do you not see all these things? Assuredly, I say to you, not one stone shall be left here upon another, that shall not be thrown down."

³ Now as He sat on the Mount of Olives, the disciples came to Him privately, saying, "Tell us, when will these things be? And what will be the sign of Your coming, and of the end of the age?"

⁴ And Jesus answered and said to them: "Take heed that no one deceives you. ⁵ For many will come in My name, saying, 'I am the Christ,' and will deceive many. ⁶ And you will hear of wars and rumors of wars. See that you are not troubled; for all these things must come

to pass, but the end is not yet. [7] For nation will rise against nation, and kingdom against kingdom. And there will be famines, pestilences, and earthquakes in various places. [8] All these are the beginning of sorrows.

[9] "Then they will deliver you up to tribulation and kill you, and you will be hated by all nations for My name's sake. [10] And then many will be offended, will betray one another, and will hate one another. [11] Then many false prophets will rise up and deceive many. [12] And because lawlessness will abound, the love of many will grow cold. [13] But he who endures to the end shall be saved. [14] And this gospel of the kingdom will be preached in all the world as a witness to all the nations, and then the end will come.

[15] "Therefore when you see the 'abomination of desolation,' spoken of by Daniel the prophet, standing in the holy place" (whoever reads, let him understand), [16] "then let those who are in Judea flee to the mountains. [17] Let him who is on the housetop not go down to take anything out of his house. [18] And let him who is in the field not go back to get his clothes. [19] But woe to those who are pregnant and to those who are nursing babies in those days! [20] And pray that your flight may not be in winter or on the Sabbath. [21] For then there will be great tribulation, such as has not been since the beginning of the world until this time, no, nor ever shall be. [22] And unless those days were shortened, no flesh would be saved; but for the elect's sake those days will be shortened.

[23] "Then if anyone says to you, 'Look, here is the Christ!' or 'There!' do not believe it. [24] For false christs and false prophets will rise and show great signs and wonders to deceive, if possible, even the elect. [25] See, I have told you beforehand.

[26] "Therefore if they say to you, 'Look, He is in the desert!' do not go out; or 'Look, He is in the inner rooms!' do not believe it. [27] For as the lightning comes from the east and flashes to the west, so also will the coming of the Son of Man be. [28] For wherever the carcass is, there the eagles will be gathered together."

3. What prediction did Jesus make about the enormous temple that the Jewish people held in such high esteem? How did the disciples respond (see verses 2–3)?

_____

_____

_____

_____

4. What are some of the warnings that Jesus gave to His followers about the coming "false christs" and "false prophets" who would try to lead them astray (see verses 4–14)?

_____

_____

_____

_____

_____

No One Knows the Day or Hour (Matthew 24:29–51)

29 "Immediately after the tribulation of those days the sun will be darkened, and the moon will not give its light; the stars will fall from heaven, and the powers of the heavens will be shaken. 30 Then the sign of the Son of Man will appear in heaven, and then all the tribes of the earth will mourn, and they will see the Son of Man coming on the clouds of heaven with power and great glory. 31 And He will send His angels with a great sound of a trumpet, and they will gather together His elect from the four winds, from one end of heaven to the other.

32 "Now learn this parable from the fig tree: When its branch has already become tender and puts forth leaves, you know that summer is near. 33 So you also, when you see all these things, know that it is near—at the doors! 34 Assuredly, I say to you, this generation will

by no means pass away till all these things take place. [35] Heaven and earth will pass away, but My words will by no means pass away."

[36] "But of that day and hour no one knows, not even the angels of heaven, but My Father only. [37] But as the days of Noah were, so also will the coming of the Son of Man be. [38] For as in the days before the flood, they were eating and drinking, marrying and giving in marriage, until the day that Noah entered the ark, [39] and did not know until the flood came and took them all away, so also will the coming of the Son of Man be. [40] Then two men will be in the field: one will be taken and the other left. [41] Two women will be grinding at the mill: one will be taken and the other left. [42] Watch therefore, for you do not know what hour your Lord is coming. [43] But know this, that if the master of the house had known what hour the thief would come, he would have watched and not allowed his house to be broken into. [44] Therefore you also be ready, for the Son of Man is coming at an hour you do not expect.

[45] "Who then is a faithful and wise servant, whom his master made ruler over his household, to give them food in due season? [46] Blessed is that servant whom his master, when he comes, will find so doing. [47] Assuredly, I say to you that he will make him ruler over all his goods. [48] But if that evil servant says in his heart, 'My master is delaying his coming,' [49] and begins to beat his fellow servants, and to eat and drink with the drunkards, [50] the master of that servant will come on a day when he is not looking for him and at an hour that he is not aware of, [51] and will cut him in two and appoint him his portion with the hypocrites. There shall be weeping and gnashing of teeth."

---

5. To what Old Testament event does Jesus compare His return (see verses 37–39)? Why do you think Jesus makes this particular comparison?

_____

_____

_____

6. Who knows the exact time of Jesus' return (see verse 36)? What does this say to us about attempting to predict the precise time of Jesus' second coming?

_____

_____

_____

_____

_____

The Parable of the Talents (Matthew 25:14–30)

14 "For the kingdom of heaven is like a man traveling to a far country, who called his own servants and delivered his goods to them. 15 And to one he gave five talents, to another two, and to another one, to each according to his own ability; and immediately he went on a journey. 16 Then he who had received the five talents went and traded with them, and made another five talents. 17 And likewise he who had received two gained two more also. 18 But he who had received one went and dug in the ground, and hid his lord's money. 19 After a long time the lord of those servants came and settled accounts with them.

20 "So he who had received five talents came and brought five other talents, saying, 'Lord, you delivered to me five talents; look, I have gained five more talents besides them.' 21 His lord said to him, 'Well done, good and faithful servant; you were faithful over a few things, I will make you ruler over many things. Enter into the joy of your lord.' 22 He also who had received two talents came and said, 'Lord, you delivered to me two talents; look, I have gained two more talents besides them.' 23 His lord said to him, 'Well done, good and faithful servant; you have been faithful over a few things, I will make you ruler over many things. Enter into the joy of your lord.'

24 "Then he who had received the one talent came and said, 'Lord, I knew you to be a hard man, reaping where you have not sown, and gathering where you have not scattered seed. 25 And I

was afraid, and went and hid your talent in the ground. Look, there you have what is yours.'

26 "But his lord answered and said to him, 'You wicked and lazy servant, you knew that I reap where I have not sown, and gather where I have not scattered seed. 27 So you ought to have deposited my money with the bankers, and at my coming I would have received back my own with interest. 28 So take the talent from him, and give it to him who has ten talents.

29 'For to everyone who has, more will be given, and he will have abundance; but from him who does not have, even what he has will be taken away. 30 And cast the unprofitable servant into the outer darkness. There will be weeping and gnashing of teeth.'"

---

7. How did the master treat the two servants who had been fruitful in his absence with the money that he had entrusted to them (see verses 21, 23)?

_____

_____

_____

_____

_____

8. The third servant not only refused to take responsibility for his failure to invest the money but also blamed the master for being "a hard man" (verse 24). How does the master respond? What does the master say the servant should have done (see verses 26–28)?

_____

_____

_____

_____

_____

REVIEWING THE STORY

Jesus turned the religious status quo of his day upside down. He turned the tables on the scribes and Pharisees, who were experts at judging others. He exposed their hypocrisy and announced their impending judgment. He turned His attention to Jerusalem, which was the center of worship in Israel, and reminded His audience of the city's history of mistreating God's prophets. He warned that the temple, the building that proclaimed Israel was God's special and holy people and the earthly place where God's presence dwelt, would soon lie in ruins.

9. What are some of the actions of the scribes and Pharisees that Jesus considered to be hypocritical (see Matthew 23:13–30)?

_____

_____

_____

_____

10. Why did Jesus give His followers a prophecy concerning His second coming (see Matthew 24:4–5)?

_____

_____

_____

11. Why should Jesus' followers live in a state of constant watchfulness and readiness (see Matthew 24:44)?

_____

_____

_____

12. What lesson did Jesus want His followers to learn from the parable of the talents (see Matthew 25:14–30)?

_____

_____

_____

_____

_____

APPLYING THE MESSAGE

13. Jesus took issue with the scribes and the Pharisees for imposing rigid laws that kept people from finding the heart of God. What are some ways you show the love of God to others? How can you better help others understand the love God has for them?

_____

_____

_____

_____

_____

_____

14. How are you staying in a state of watchfulness as you wait for Jesus' return? How are you using the gifts that God has entrusted to you to advance His kingdom?

_____

_____

_____

_____

_____

Reflecting on the Meaning

Jesus' return is usually described as a terrifying day of judgment—an event we should all fear. However, for Christians, Jesus' return is a source of hope, anticipation, and motivation. Jesus' second coming is when He will end the terrible Tribulation period. When He returns, we will enter into the millennium—a 1,000-year period of peace and prosperity!

However, while we wait, we work. There are people God wants us to invite into His family so they can be part of His kingdom. Plus, the work we do now—the way we love, serve, and grow—prepares us for what we will do in God's kingdom when Jesus returns. His return in the future motivates us to work in the present.

The imminence of Jesus' return adds urgency to our discipleship and service. We don't have the luxury of waiting for the "right" time to put our spiritual gifts to work. None of us knows just how much time we have to work with because none of us knows when Jesus will return. So, while we wait, we work. We anticipate Jesus' return in the future and work to build His kingdom in the present.

Journaling Your Response

What feelings arise within you when you consider Jesus' second coming? Why?

THE DARKEST DAY

Matthew 26:1–27:44

GETTING STARTED

What would you describe as being the "darkest days" in your life? How were you able to get through that difficult time?

_____

_____

_____

_____

_____

_____

_____

_____

_____

_____

_____

_____

_____

_____

_____

_____

_____

_____

_____

_____

_____

SETTING THE STAGE

Jesus always knew the climax of His ministry would be His death, and that it would serve as the centerpiece of God's plan to rescue humanity from the power of sin and the evil one. During Jesus' life, He repeatedly told His disciples that He would have to die, but they took it as another case of Him speaking in parables. The topic left them confused. In fact, as we have seen, Peter one time even went so far as to rebuke Jesus for predicting His death and said he would never let that happen to his Lord. His comments didn't go over well.

Jesus' disciples were understandably uneasy about His repeated mentions of His death. Again, remember that in first-century Israel, what happened to those who claimed to be a "messiah" usually happened to their followers. However, Jesus kept speaking and teaching about His death . . . and the disciples remained confused. Even after giving one final hint, in which Jesus plainly stated, "You know that after two days is the Passover, and the Son of Man will be delivered up to be crucified" (Matthew 26:2), the disciples were still stunned when their Lord was arrested and taken to be crucified. They never saw it coming.

Chaos ensued when He was led away. Promises of loyalty and protection made in the safety of a private room were quickly broken. Jesus' closest companions fled. Peter denied that he even knew Jesus. At His trial, Jesus faced His enemies alone. The Pharisees got the verdict they wanted and put an end to Jesus' constant provocation. Jesus hung on the cross . . . to them just another pretender and another failed messiah. It seemed as if evil had won.

EXPLORING THE TEXT

The Plot to Kill Jesus (Matthew 26:1–25)

> [1] Now it came to pass, when Jesus had finished all these sayings, that He said to His disciples, [2] "You know that after two days is the Passover, and the Son of Man will be delivered up to be crucified."

³ Then the chief priests, the scribes, and the elders of the people assembled at the palace of the high priest, who was called Caiaphas, ⁴ and plotted to take Jesus by trickery and kill Him. ⁵ But they said, "Not during the feast, lest there be an uproar among the people."

⁶ And when Jesus was in Bethany at the house of Simon the leper, ⁷ a woman came to Him having an alabaster flask of very costly fragrant oil, and she poured it on His head as He sat at the table. ⁸ But when His disciples saw it, they were indignant, saying, "Why this waste? ⁹ For this fragrant oil might have been sold for much and given to the poor."

¹⁰ But when Jesus was aware of it, He said to them, "Why do you trouble the woman? For she has done a good work for Me. ¹¹ For you have the poor with you always, but Me you do not have always. ¹² For in pouring this fragrant oil on My body, she did it for My burial. ¹³ Assuredly, I say to you, wherever this gospel is preached in the whole world, what this woman has done will also be told as a memorial to her."

¹⁴ Then one of the twelve, called Judas Iscariot, went to the chief priests ¹⁵ and said, "What are you willing to give me if I deliver Him to you?" And they counted out to him thirty pieces of silver. ¹⁶ So from that time he sought opportunity to betray Him.

¹⁷ Now on the first day of the Feast of the Unleavened Bread the disciples came to Jesus, saying to Him, "Where do You want us to prepare for You to eat the Passover?"

¹⁸ And He said, "Go into the city to a certain man, and say to him, 'The Teacher says, "My time is at hand; I will keep the Passover at your house with My disciples." ' "

¹⁹ So the disciples did as Jesus had directed them; and they prepared the Passover.

²⁰ When evening had come, He sat down with the twelve. ²¹ Now as they were eating, He said, "Assuredly, I say to you, one of you will betray Me."

²² And they were exceedingly sorrowful, and each of them began to say to Him, "Lord, is it I?"

²³ He answered and said, "He who dipped his hand with Me in the dish will betray Me. ²⁴ The Son of Man indeed goes just as it is written of Him, but woe to that man by whom the Son of Man is betrayed! It would have been good for that man if he had not been born."

²⁵ Then Judas, who was betraying Him, answered and said, "Rabbi, is it I?"

He said to him, "You have said it."

---

1. Why did the chief priests and elders want to wait until after the Passover festival to make their move against Jesus (see verse 5)?

_____

_____

_____

_____

_____

2. How did the disciples react to the woman pouring a jar of expensive oil on Jesus' head? Why were they upset? What did Jesus say the woman was actually doing (see verses 8–12)?

_____

_____

_____

_____

_____

The Prayer in the Garden (Matthew 26:36–56)

³⁶ Then Jesus came with them to a place called Gethsemane, and said to the disciples, "Sit here while I go and pray over there." ³⁷ And He took with Him Peter and the two sons of Zebedee, and He began to be

sorrowful and deeply distressed. [38] Then He said to them, "My soul is exceedingly sorrowful, even to death. Stay here and watch with Me."

[39] He went a little farther and fell on His face, and prayed, saying, "O My Father, if it is possible, let this cup pass from Me; nevertheless, not as I will, but as You will."

[40] Then He came to the disciples and found them sleeping, and said to Peter, "What! Could you not watch with Me one hour? [41] Watch and pray, lest you enter into temptation. The spirit indeed is willing, but the flesh is weak."

[42] Again, a second time, He went away and prayed, saying, "O My Father, if this cup cannot pass away from Me unless I drink it, Your will be done." [43] And He came and found them asleep again, for their eyes were heavy.

[44] So He left them, went away again, and prayed the third time, saying the same words. [45] Then He came to His disciples and said to them, "Are you still sleeping and resting? Behold, the hour is at hand, and the Son of Man is being betrayed into the hands of sinners. [46] Rise, let us be going. See, My betrayer is at hand."

[47] And while He was still speaking, behold, Judas, one of the twelve, with a great multitude with swords and clubs, came from the chief priests and elders of the people.

[48] Now His betrayer had given them a sign, saying, "Whomever I kiss, He is the One; seize Him." [49] Immediately he went up to Jesus and said, "Greetings, Rabbi!" and kissed Him.

[50] But Jesus said to him, "Friend, why have you come?"

Then they came and laid hands on Jesus and took Him. [51] And suddenly, one of those who were with Jesus stretched out his hand and drew his sword, struck the servant of the high priest, and cut off his ear.

[52] But Jesus said to him, "Put your sword in its place, for all who take the sword will perish by the sword. [53] Or do you think that I cannot now pray to My Father, and He will provide Me with more than twelve legions of angels? [54] How then could the Scriptures be fulfilled, that it must happen thus?"

⁵⁵ In that hour Jesus said to the multitudes, "Have you come out, as against a robber, with swords and clubs to take Me? I sat daily with you, teaching in the temple, and you did not seize Me. ⁵⁶ But all this was done that the Scriptures of the prophets might be fulfilled."

Then all the disciples forsook Him and fled.

---

3. What request did Jesus make of His Father in prayer (see verses 39, 42)? Why do you think He made this request?

_____

_____

_____

_____

_____

4. How did Jesus' disciples fail Him, both in the Garden of Gethsemane during His time of need, and after His arrest (see verses 40–48, 56)?

_____

_____

_____

_____

_____

Peter Denies Knowing Jesus (Matthew 26:57–75)

⁵⁷ And those who had laid hold of Jesus led Him away to Caiaphas the high priest, where the scribes and the elders were assembled. ⁵⁸ But Peter followed Him at a distance to the high priest's courtyard. And he went in and sat with the servants to see the end.

⁵⁹ Now the chief priests, the elders, and all the council sought false testimony against Jesus to put Him to death, ⁶⁰ but found none. Even though many false witnesses came forward, they found none.

But at last two false witnesses came forward [61] and said, "This fellow said, 'I am able to destroy the temple of God and to build it in three days.' "

[62] And the high priest arose and said to Him, "Do You answer nothing? What is it these men testify against You?" [63] But Jesus kept silent. And the high priest answered and said to Him, "I put You under oath by the living God: Tell us if You are the Christ, the Son of God!"

[64] Jesus said to him, "It is as you said. Nevertheless, I say to you, hereafter you will see the Son of Man sitting at the right hand of the Power, and coming on the clouds of heaven."

[65] Then the high priest tore his clothes, saying, "He has spoken blasphemy! What further need do we have of witnesses? Look, now you have heard His blasphemy! [66] What do you think?"

They answered and said, "He is deserving of death."

[67] Then they spat in His face and beat Him; and others struck Him with the palms of their hands, [68] saying, "Prophesy to us, Christ! Who is the one who struck You?"

[69] Now Peter sat outside in the courtyard. And a servant girl came to him, saying, "You also were with Jesus of Galilee."

[70] But he denied it before them all, saying, "I do not know what you are saying."

[71] And when he had gone out to the gateway, another girl saw him and said to those who were there, "This fellow also was with Jesus of Nazareth."

[72] But again he denied with an oath, "I do not know the Man!"

[73] And a little later those who stood by came up and said to Peter, "Surely you also are one of them, for your speech betrays you."

[74] Then he began to curse and swear, saying, "I do not know the Man!"

Immediately a rooster crowed. [75] And Peter remembered the word of Jesus who had said to him, "Before the rooster crows, you will deny Me three times." So he went out and wept bitterly.

5. What tactics did the council employ to try to find cause to put Jesus to death? What ultimately caused them to rule that He was deserving of execution (see verses 59–66)?

_____

_____

_____

_____

_____

_____

_____

6. Earlier that day, Peter had told Jesus that "even if all are made to stumble because of You, I will never be made to stumble" (Matthew 26:33). What do you think caused Peter to so quickly go back on this promise—not once but *three* times?

_____

_____

_____

_____

_____

_____

_____

_____

The King on a Cross (Matthew 27:27–44)

27 Then the soldiers of the governor took Jesus into the Praetorium and gathered the whole garrison around Him. 28 And they stripped Him and put a scarlet robe on Him. 29 When they had twisted a crown of thorns, they put it on His head, and a reed in His right hand. And they

bowed the knee before Him and mocked Him, saying, "Hail, King of the Jews!" [30] Then they spat on Him, and took the reed and struck Him on the head. [31] And when they had mocked Him, they took the robe off Him, put His own clothes on Him, and led Him away to be crucified.

[32] Now as they came out, they found a man of Cyrene, Simon by name. Him they compelled to bear His cross. [33] And when they had come to a place called Golgotha, that is to say, Place of a Skull, [34] they gave Him sour wine mingled with gall to drink. But when He had tasted it, He would not drink.

[35] Then they crucified Him, and divided His garments, casting lots, that it might be fulfilled which was spoken by the prophet:

"They divided My garments among them,
And for My clothing they cast lots."

[36] Sitting down, they kept watch over Him there. [37] And they put up over His head the accusation written against Him:

THIS IS JESUS THE KING OF THE JEWS.

[38] Then two robbers were crucified with Him, one on the right and another on the left.

[39] And those who passed by blasphemed Him, wagging their heads [40] and saying, "You who destroy the temple and build it in three days, save Yourself! If You are the Son of God, come down from the cross." [41] Likewise the chief priests also, mocking with the scribes and elders, said, [42] "He saved others; Himself He cannot save. If He is the King of Israel, let Him now come down from the cross, and we will believe Him. [43] He trusted in God; let Him deliver Him now if He will have Him; for He said, 'I am the Son of God.' "

[44] Even the robbers who were crucified with Him reviled Him with the same thing.

7. According to Luke's Gospel, when Pilate (the Roman governor of Judea) asked Christ if He was the King of the Jews, Jesus replied, "It is as you say" (23:3). How did the Roman soldiers mock Jesus' claim of kingship in this passage (see Matthew 27:28–31, 37)?

_____

_____

_____

_____

_____

_____

8. What did the people say that Jesus would have to do for them to believe that He was the Messiah and the Son of God (see verses 42–43)?

_____

_____

_____

_____

_____

_____

_____

REVIEWING THE STORY

Only Jesus truly understood what took place during His arrest, trial, and crucifixion. His enemies believed they had outmaneuvered Him with their plotting and treachery. His disciples mistook Mary's burial anointing for a waste of expensive oil and believed they would remain faithful to Him to the end. Pontius Pilate believed he held Jesus' fate in his hands. Roman soldiers, and one of the criminals crucified with Him, believed He was just another failed rebel. The witnesses to His crucifixion believed that His death was the end of His story. They were all wrong.

9. What deal did Judas Iscariot make with the chief priests (see Matthew 26:14–16)?

_____

_____

_____

_____

_____

_____

_____

10. How did Jesus respond when Peter tried to protect Him (see Matthew 26:52–54)?

_____

_____

_____

_____

_____

_____

11. How did Peter's denials of Jesus escalate each time he was questioned? What caused Peter to recall Jesus' words to him (see Matthew 26:69–75)?

_____

_____

_____

_____

_____

_____

12. What are some of the ways the people mocked Jesus as He hung on the cross (see Matthew 27:39–44)?

_____

_____

_____

_____

_____

_____

_____

_____

_____

APPLYING THE MESSAGE

13. Has there ever been a time when you didn't want people to know that you followed Jesus? What happened? How did you respond?

_____

_____

_____

_____

_____

_____

_____

_____

_____

14. Has there ever been a time when God's teachings or actions made you uncomfortable? What happened? How did that change your relationship with Him?

_____

_____

_____

_____

_____

_____

_____

_____

REFLECTING ON THE MEANING

The cross was a symbol of power. It communicated one thing . . . and only one thing: Rome was all-powerful and couldn't be beaten. Any attempt to challenge Rome would end in one place—the cross. The cross was proof that Rome was the ultimate power in the world.

The cross protected the power of Rome. Any attempt to stand up to Rome's power was met with violence, force, and humiliation. It was a place of suffering, death, and despair. It was evil, the product of a twisted human mind that used its creativity to invent a method of killing so torturous it required a new way to describe the pain it caused: _excruciating_.

When the Romans crucified Jesus, they intended to send a message. Jesus thought He was a king . . . thought He had power . . . thought He could challenge Rome . . . yet He still wound up on a cross, just like so many other failed revolutionaries that came before Him. The cross was supposed to prove that Jesus was just another man, powerless in the face of evil.

However, that's not what happened. At the cross, Jesus allowed Rome to unleash all of its power, violence, oppression, and brutality upon Him.

Evil had every chance to prove it was unstoppable, unconquerable. But it failed. All of Rome's power, all the horror of the cross, couldn't stop God's power. The power of sin, evil, and death couldn't defeat the power of the One who created the universe. Evil itself was defeated. The cross didn't have the final word.

Jesus' resurrection transformed history and launched a revolution—a new way of being human—that carries on through our lives today. Not only did Jesus transform history, but He also transformed the cross from a place of death and despair to a symbol of hope and victory!

JOURNALING YOUR RESPONSE

What would it look like for Jesus to bring victory over sin, evil, and death in your life? How would it transform your relationship with God and with other people?

HE IS RISEN INDEED

Matthew 27:45–28:20

GETTING STARTED

When is a time in your life that you received an incredible surprise? What happened?

_____

_____

_____

_____

_____

_____

_____

_____

_____

_____

_____

_____

_____

_____

_____

_____

_____

_____

_____

SETTING THE STAGE

The cross is the symbol of Jesus' victory over sin, evil, and death. But without the empty tomb, the cross is meaningless. Without the resurrection, Jesus is just another misunderstood religious teacher, another failed revolutionary, another ordinary human.

After all, ordinary humans die . . . and stay dead. This had been true since the first man and first woman died. So it was that everyone who watched Jesus die—His disciples, the Pharisees, the Roman soldiers, and the crowds who witnessed His execution—knew that His death was the end of the story. Dead people don't come back to life.

Yet Jesus was no ordinary human. The resurrection proved that He was the One whom He claimed to be: a King who ruled over all creation and was more powerful than sin, death, and evil. The disciples who saw the risen Jesus knew this signaled the beginning of something radically different—a totally new way of understanding God, the world, and humanity.

The resurrection was proof that death no longer had the final word in human existence. What humans had spent their lives trying to avoid—what humans considered the ultimate power—did not have the final say. God had kept His promises to His people! Death itself had been defeated, and a whole new way of living had been unlocked for all humanity.

EXPLORING THE TEXT

Jesus Dies on the Cross (Matthew 27:45–56)

[45] Now from the sixth hour until the ninth hour there was darkness over all the land. [46] And about the ninth hour Jesus cried out with a loud voice, saying, "Eli, Eli, lama sabachthani?" that is, "My God, My God, why have You forsaken Me?"

[47] Some of those who stood there, when they heard that, said, "This Man is calling for Elijah!" [48] Immediately one of them ran and

took a sponge, filled it with sour wine and put it on a reed, and offered it to Him to drink.

[49] The rest said, "Let Him alone; let us see if Elijah will come to save Him."

[50] And Jesus cried out again with a loud voice, and yielded up His spirit.

[51] Then, behold, the veil of the temple was torn in two from top to bottom; and the earth quaked, and the rocks were split, [52] and the graves were opened; and many bodies of the saints who had fallen asleep were raised; [53] and coming out of the graves after His resurrection, they went into the holy city and appeared to many.

[54] So when the centurion and those with him, who were guarding Jesus, saw the earthquake and the things that had happened, they feared greatly, saying, "Truly this was the Son of God!"

[55] And many women who followed Jesus from Galilee, ministering to Him, were there looking on from afar, [56] among whom were Mary Magdalene, Mary the mother of James and Joses, and the mother of Zebedee's sons.

---

1. A Jewish tradition held that Elijah would come and rescue the righteous in their time of distress. How does this explain the people's misperception that Jesus was calling for Elijah as He hung on the cross (see verses 47–49)?

----

2. What caused the Roman centurion to call Jesus "the Son of God" (verse 54)?

_____

_____

_____

_____

_____

_____

_____

_____

Jesus Is Buried (Matthew 27:57–66)

57 Now when evening had come, there came a rich man from Arimathea, named Joseph, who himself had also become a disciple of Jesus. 58 This man went to Pilate and asked for the body of Jesus. Then Pilate commanded the body to be given to him. 59 When Joseph had taken the body, he wrapped it in a clean linen cloth, 60 and laid it in his new tomb which he had hewn out of the rock; and he rolled a large stone against the door of the tomb, and departed. 61 And Mary Magdalene was there, and the other Mary, sitting opposite the tomb.

62 On the next day, which followed the Day of Preparation, the chief priests and Pharisees gathered together to Pilate, 63 saying, "Sir, we remember, while He was still alive, how that deceiver said, 'After three days I will rise.' 64 Therefore command that the tomb be made secure until the third day, lest His disciples come by night and steal Him away, and say to the people, 'He has risen from the dead.' So the last deception will be worse than the first."

65 Pilate said to them, "You have a guard; go your way, make it as secure as you know how." 66 So they went and made the tomb secure, sealing the stone and setting the guard.

3. How did Jesus' body come to be placed in the tomb of Joseph of Arimathea? What precautions did Joseph take to secure the body (see verses 57–60)?

_____

_____

_____

_____

4. Which of Jesus' teachings did the chief priests and Pharisees remember that His disciples forgot (see verse 63)? What actions did the religious leaders take as a result?

_____

_____

_____

_____

The Empty Tomb (Matthew 28:1–10)

¹ Now after the Sabbath, as the first day of the week began to dawn, Mary Magdalene and the other Mary came to see the tomb. ² And behold, there was a great earthquake; for an angel of the Lord descended from heaven, and came and rolled back the stone from the door, and sat on it. ³ His countenance was like lightning, and his clothing as white as snow. ⁴ And the guards shook for fear of him, and became like dead men.

⁵ But the angel answered and said to the women, "Do not be afraid, for I know that you seek Jesus who was crucified. ⁶ He is not here; for He is risen, as He said. Come, see the place where the Lord lay. ⁷ And go quickly and tell His disciples that He is risen from the dead, and indeed He is going before you into Galilee; there you will see Him. Behold, I have told you."

⁸ So they went out quickly from the tomb with fear and great joy, and ran to bring His disciples word.

⁹ And as they went to tell His disciples, behold, Jesus met them, saying, "Rejoice!" So they came and held Him by the feet and worshiped Him. ¹⁰ Then Jesus said to them, "Do not be afraid. Go and tell My brethren to go to Galilee, and there they will see Me."

---

5. What did the guards witness on the morning of Jesus' resurrection? How did they respond (see verses 2–4)?

_____

_____

_____

_____

6. How did the women respond when they saw the angel? What instructions did the angel give to them (see verses 5–8)?

_____

_____

_____

_____

The Great Commission (Matthew 28:11–20)

---

¹¹ Now while they were going, behold, some of the guard came into the city and reported to the chief priests all the things that had happened. ¹² When they had assembled with the elders and consulted together, they gave a large sum of money to the soldiers, ¹³ saying, "Tell them, 'His disciples came at night and stole Him away while we slept.' ¹⁴ And if this comes to the governor's ears, we will appease him and make you secure." ¹⁵ So they took the money and did as they were instructed; and this saying is commonly reported among the Jews until this day.

¹⁶Then the eleven disciples went away into Galilee, to the mountain which Jesus had appointed for them. ¹⁷When they saw Him, they worshiped Him; but some doubted.

¹⁸And Jesus came and spoke to them, saying, "All authority has been given to Me in heaven and on earth. ¹⁹Go therefore and make disciples of all the nations, baptizing them in the name of the Father and of the Son and of the Holy Spirit, ²⁰teaching them to observe all things that I have commanded you; and lo, I am with you always, even to the end of the age." Amen.

---

7. Why do you think the chief priests went to such trouble to cover up the truth about Jesus' resurrection? Why did the soldiers go along with the chief priests' plan (see verses 12–15)?

_____

_____

_____

_____

_____

_____

8. What were Jesus' final instructions to His followers? What promise did He make to them (see verses 18–20)?

_____

_____

_____

_____

_____

REVIEWING THE STORY

Jesus' resurrection inspired a variety of reactions from those who witnessed it. The Roman guards who kept watch over Jesus' tomb collapsed in fear when they saw the angel. Mary Magdalene and "the other Mary" left His empty tomb overcome with fear and joy. When they encountered the risen Jesus, they fell at his feet and worshiped Him. The chief priests plotted and concocted a lie to try to explain it away. The disciples' responses were split. Some believed and worshiped Him, while others had their doubts.

9. The veil in the temple separated the Holy of Holies—the earthly dwelling place of God's presence—from the rest of the temple. Given this, what is the significance of this veil being torn in two at the moment of Jesus' death (see Matthew 27:51)?

_____

_____

_____

_____

10. Three words in Matthew 28:6 suggest that Jesus' resurrection should not have been a surprise to His followers. What are they? Why are they significant?

_____

_____

_____

_____

11. How did the chief priests want the Roman soldiers to explain the empty tomb (see Matthew 28:11–14)?

_____

_____

_____

_____

12. The first and last sentences of Jesus' instructions to His followers in Matthew 28:18–20 should fill us with confidence as we fulfill His commission. What are they?

_____

_____

_____

APPLYING THE MESSAGE

13. What does the empty tomb mean for you as a follower of Christ?

_____

_____

_____

14. What does it look like for you to go and teach others what Jesus has taught you?

_____

_____

_____

REFLECTING ON THE MEANING

Jesus' resurrection gave His followers *a new start*. The disciples had failed spectacularly after they shared the Passover meal together. Judas Iscariot had agreed to turn Jesus over to His enemies. Peter, James, and John had fallen asleep after Jesus asked them to keep watch while He prayed. On three separate occasions, Peter denied even *knowing* Jesus. The others scattered. Imagine the guilt and shame they felt after Jesus' death. His resurrection gave them a chance to make things right—to receive forgiveness and redemption.

Jesus' resurrection gave His followers *a new enemy*. Rome allowed a certain measure of religious freedom throughout the empire . . . unless that religion threatened its stability. With Jewish religious leaders whispering in their ears, Roman authorities became convinced that Christianity posed a threat. So they began to persecute Jesus' followers.

Jesus' resurrection gave His followers *a new purpose*. They had good news to spread throughout the world: *Jesus is risen! The power of sin and death is broken! Everyone who believes Jesus is the Messiah and follows Him will have eternal life!*

Jesus' resurrection gave His followers *new courage*. Since Jesus had defeated death, they no longer had anything to fear. The worst their enemies could do was to kill them. Death now meant eternal life.

What was true for the disciples is true for us today. Jesus' victory over sin and death means we don't have to carry the mistakes and failures of our past. When we believe in Jesus and decide to follow Him, we're forgiven—released from all our guilt and shame. We will face opposition—and some of it will be intense—but we can know with confidence that the King who gave us that assignment has already conquered every obstacle we will ever face.

JOURNALING YOUR RESPONSE

How would your life be different if Jesus hadn't come back from the dead? How has His resurrection given you a new life?

_____

_____

_____

_____

_____

_____

_____

_____

_____

_____

LEADER'S GUIDE

Thank you for choosing to lead your group through this study from Dr. David Jeremiah on *The Gospel of Matthew*. Being a group leader has its own rewards, and it is our prayer that your walk with the Lord will deepen through this experience. During the twelve lessons in this study, you and your group will read selected passages from Matthew, explore key themes in the Gospel based on teachings from Dr. Jeremiah, and review questions that will encourage group discussion. There are multiple components in this section that can help you structure your lessons and discussion time, so please be sure to read and consider each one.

BEFORE YOU BEGIN

Before your first meeting, make sure you and your group are well-versed with the content of the lesson. Group members should have their own copy of *The Gospel of Matthew* study guide prior to the first meeting so they can follow along and record their answers, thoughts, and insights. After the first week, you may wish to assign the study guide lesson as homework prior to the group meeting and then use the meeting time to discuss the content in the lesson.

To ensure everyone has a chance to participate in the discussion, the ideal size for a group is around eight to ten people. If there are more than ten people, break up the bigger group into smaller subgroups. Make sure the members are committed to participating each week, as this will help create stability and help you better prepare the structure of the meeting.

At the beginning of each week's study, start with the opening Getting Started question to introduce the topic you will be discussing. The members should answer briefly, as the goal is just for them to have an idea of the subject in their minds as you go over the lesson. This will allow the members to become engaged and ready to interact with the rest of the group.

After reviewing the lesson, try to initiate a free-flowing discussion. Invite group members to bring questions and insights they may have discovered to the next meeting, especially if they were unsure of the meaning of some parts of the lesson. Be prepared to discuss how biblical truth applies to the world we live in today.

WEEKLY PREPARATION

As the group leader, here are a few things you can do to prepare for each meeting:

- *Be thoroughly familiar with the material in the lesson.* Make sure you understand the content of each lesson so you know how to structure the group time and are prepared to lead the group discussion.

- *Decide, ahead of time, which questions you want to discuss.* Depending on how much time you have each week, you may not be able to reflect on every question. Select specific questions that you feel will evoke the best discussion.

- *Take prayer requests.* At the end of your discussion, take prayer requests from your group members and then pray for one another.

STRUCTURING THE DISCUSSION TIME

There are several ways to structure the duration of the study. You can choose to cover each lesson individually, for a total of twelve weeks of group meetings, or you can combine two lessons together per week, for a total of six weeks of group meetings. You can also have the group members read just the selected passages of Scripture that are given in each lesson, or they can cover the entire Gospel of Matthew. The following charts illustrates these options:

TWELVE-WEEK FORMAT

Week	Lessons Covered	Expanded Reading
1	The Making of a Messiah	*Matthew 1:1–2:23*
2	The Start of Something Big	*Matthew 3:1–4:25*
3	The Sermon on the Mount	*Matthew 5:1–7:29*
4	Who Is This Man?	*Matthew 8:1–9:38*
5	Sheep, Snakes, and Doves	*Matthew 10:1–12:50*
6	The Greatest Stories Ever Told	*Matthew 13:1–15:39*
7	"Who Do You Say I Am?"	*Matthew 16:1–17:27*
8	Redefining Greatness	*Matthew 18:1–20:34*
9	The Arrival of the King	*Matthew 21:1–22:46*
10	Jesus Prepares His Followers	*Matthew 23:1–25:46*
11	The Darkest Day	*Matthew 26:1–27:44*
12	He Is Risen Indeed	*Matthew 27:45–28:20*

SIX-WEEK FORMAT

Week	Lessons Covered	Expanded Reading
1	The Making of a Messiah / The Start of Something Big	*Matthew 1:1–4:25*
2	The Sermon on the Mount / Who Is This Man?	*Matthew 5:1–9:38*
3	Sheep, Snakes, and Doves / The Greatest Stories Ever Told	*Matthew 10:1–15:39*
4	"Who Do You Say I Am?" / Redefining Greatness	*Matthew 16:1–20:34*
5	The Arrival of the King / Jesus Prepares His Followers	*Matthew 21:1–25:46*
6	The Darkest Day / He Is Risen Indeed	*Matthew 26:1–28:20*

In regard to organizing your time when planning your group Bible study, the following two schedules, for sixty minutes and ninety minutes, can give you a structure for the lesson:

Section	60 Minutes	90 Minutes
Welcome: Members arrive and get settled	5 minutes	10 minutes
Getting Started Question: Prepares the group for interacting with one another	10 minutes	10 minutes
Message: Review the lesson	15 minutes	25 minutes
Discussion: Discuss questions in the lesson	25 minutes	35 minutes
Review and Prayer: Review the key points of the lesson and have a closing time of prayer	5 minutes	10 minutes

As the group leader, it is up to you to keep track of the time and keep things moving according to your schedule. If your group is having a good discussion, don't feel the need to stop and move on to the next question. Remember, the purpose is to pull together ideas and share unique insights on the lesson. Encourage everyone to participate, but don't be concerned if certain group members are more quiet. They may just be internally reflecting on the questions and need time to process their ideas before they can share them.

GROUP DYNAMICS

Leading a group study can be a rewarding experience for you and your group members—but that doesn't mean there won't be challenges. Certain members may feel uncomfortable discussing topics that they consider very personal and might be afraid of being called on. Some members might have disagreements on specific issues. To help prevent these scenarios, consider the following ground rules:

- If someone has a question that may seem off topic, suggest that it is discussed at another time, or ask the group if they are okay with addressing that topic.

- If someone asks a question you don't know the answer to, confess that you don't know and move on. If you feel comfortable, invite other group members to give their opinions or share their comments based on personal experience.
- If you feel like a couple of people are talking much more than others, direct questions to people who may not have shared yet. You could even ask the more dominating members to help draw out the quiet ones.
- When there is a disagreement, encourage the group members to process the matter in love. Invite members from opposing sides to evaluate their opinions and consider the ideas of the other members. Lead the group through Scripture that addresses the topic, and look for common ground.

When issues arise, encourage your group to think of Scripture: "Love one another" (John 13:34), "If it is possible, as much as it depends on you, live peaceably with all men" (Romans 12:18), and, "Be swift to hear, slow to speak, slow to wrath" (James 1:19).

ABOUT
Dr. David Jeremiah and Turning Point

Dr. David Jeremiah is the founder of Turning Point, a ministry committed to providing Christians with sound Bible teaching relevant to today's changing times through radio and television broadcasts, audio series, books, and live events. Dr. Jeremiah's teaching on topics such as family, prayer, worship, angels, and biblical prophecy forms the foundation of Turning Point.

David and his wife, Donna, reside in El Cajon, California, where he serves as the senior pastor of Shadow Mountain Community Church. David and Donna have four children and twelve grandchildren.

In 1982, Dr. Jeremiah brought the same solid teaching to San Diego television that he shares weekly with his congregation. Shortly thereafter, Turning Point expanded its ministry to radio. Dr. Jeremiah's inspiring messages can now be heard worldwide on radio, television, and the internet.

Because Dr. Jeremiah desires to know his listening audience, he travels nationwide holding ministry rallies and spiritual enrichment conferences that touch the hearts and lives of many people. According to Dr. Jeremiah, "At some point in time, everyone reaches a turning point; and for every person, that moment is unique, an experience to hold onto forever. There's so much changing in today's world that sometimes it's difficult to choose the right path. Turning Point offers people an understanding of God's Word and seeks to make a difference in their lives."

Dr. Jeremiah has authored numerous books, including *Escape the Coming Night* (Revelation), *The Handwriting on the Wall* (Daniel), *Overcoming Loneliness, Prayer—The Great Adventure, God in You* (Holy Spirit), *When*

Your World Falls Apart, Slaying the Giants in Your Life, My Heart's Desire, Hope for Today, Captured by Grace, Signs of Life, What in the World Is Going On?, The Coming Economic Armageddon, I Never Thought I'd See the Day!, God Loves You: He Always Has—He Always Will, Agents of the Apocalypse, Agents of Babylon, Revealing the Mysteries of Heaven, People Are Asking . . . Is This the End?, A Life Beyond Amazing, Overcomer, and *The Book of Signs.*